Stories
Japanese Tea

Stories of Japanese Tea

The Regions, the Growers, and the Craft

Zach Mangan

FOREWORD *by* DAVID BOULEY

PRINCETON ARCHITECTURAL PRESS · NEW YORK

Published by
Princeton Architectural Press
70 West 36th Street
New York, NY 10018
www.papress.com

© 2022 Zach Mangan
All rights reserved.
Printed and bound in China
25 24 23 22   4 3 2 1 First edition

ISBN 978-1-64896-007-9

Production Editor: Kristen Hewitt
Designer: Paula Baver

Image Credits:
p. 172: Photograph by AJ Meeker
All other photographs by Zach Mangan

Library of Congress Control Number: 2021948261

Thank you to my wife, Minami, my family, and all those who work day in, day out to create the beautiful world of Japanese tea.

Though I sweep and sweep,
Everywhere my garden path,
Though invisible
On the slim pine needles still
Specks of dirt may yet be found.

—

When you take a sip
From the bowl of powder Tea
There within it lies
Clear reflected in its depths
Blue of sky and grey of sea.

— Sen no Rikyū

CONTENTS

FOREWORD

I MET ZACH IN THE SUMMER OF 2011, JUST AFTER OPENING THE kaiseki restaurant Brushstroke in partnership with Osaka's renowned Tsuji Culinary Institute. The respect for seasonality and craft I observed in Japanese cooking agreed with my own approach to food, as a chef raised on a farm who dedicated his career to nouvelle cuisine. Brushstroke was a partnership aimed at sharing the rich history of kaiseki-style cuisine: sharing the rhythm and flavor of the seasons, the seamlessness of a style of eating that is both delicious and healthy, and the building of a template to explore the intersection of food, wine, sake, and of course, tea. When I first met Zach, I had just returned from Kyoto, where I had the good fortune of attending a traditional Japanese tea ceremony hosted by a two hundred-year-old wagashi maker. When Zach produced a bag full of Japanese teas that rivaled the best I had tasted in my own travels, it was clear that he was uniquely knowledgeable and passionate. Immediately after our first tasting, I shook his hand and offered him the task of building Brushstroke's tea menu. I kept a close eye on its development during my daily ritual of walking over each day from the kitchen of Bouley to make myself a cup of tea at Brushstroke. With each day it was clear that Zach's passion reflected my same ideals.

Throughout our time together at Brushstroke and Bouley at Home, Zach and I have presented tea-pairing dinners, tasted award-winning teas, and discussed obsessively how terroir, varietal, and a farmer's point of view so profoundly impact a cup of tea. Zach approaches tea like a respected wine importer: building relationships with the finest growers, learning and sharing their stories, and advocating on their behalf. And he has elevated tea to a status usually reserved for wine; I am now free to appreciate the subtle craft of how a sencha from Kagoshima Prefecture was made, as though it were a pinot noir from Burgundy or a fine Sancerre.

Zach and I have shared ideas about how to shed more light on the remarkable world of Japanese tea. Our goal is the same; as Zach says, "In the end, sharing the stories and deeper details of the teas allows our customers to gain the confidence to make choices about what they like based on taste. Being guided by their palate allows them to avoid falling prey to the marketing hype that is still so pervasive in a young industry like specialty tea." It is truly my hope that those of you reading this book will follow your curiosity and Zach's lead. I assure you that what lies ahead is revelatory: The world of tea is truly incredible, and all of us have a place in it.

David Bouley
Connecticut, March 2021

David Bouley is an American chef and restaurateur with restaurants in Tribeca, New York City. He is best known for his flagship restaurant, Bouley.

Sencha from Shizuoka Prefecture

INTRODUCTION

I OFTEN GET ASKED WHY I DECIDED, AT TWENTY-FOUR, TO TAKE a detour from my life in music and begin pursuing a career in Japanese tea. The truth is, at the time, I didn't exactly know I was doing that. I did know that ever since my first encounter with Japanese tea, I had found it delicious and fulfilling. The aroma especially intrigued me. I first experienced fresh Japanese tea in Paris while on tour with my band. I bought a small bag of shincha, the coveted first spring harvest, from a shop in Le Marais. The smell of the glossy, needlelike leaves was incredibly nostalgic, though I had never experienced it before. It reminded me of the lawn of my childhood home when freshly mowed. I brewed it and was captivated by how much flavor was packed inside my tiny cup of tea. Before I knew anything about what I was tasting, I loved it. Texture, aroma, sweetness, the savory tang of umami. It was a complete experience—fortifying for the body and stimulating for the mind. Little did I know, this would be a life-changing experience.

My love for Japanese tea grew, and I began to search for it back in the United States. But what I found in tea shops, specialty stores, and even online was nothing like what I had experienced in France. And what's more, I noticed that shops selling teas with less aroma, flavor, and depth seemed content to do so—blissfully unaware of how delicious fresh Japanese tea could be. It was depressing to search out, purchase, then taste disappointing tea after disappointing tea. None of it had the lift or depth of the cup that now lived in my memory.

After months of searching, I finally found Ito En, a shop in New York City selling teas from throughout Japan; these were labeled with the Japanese prefecture from which they hailed and detailed tasting notes. When I visited the store there was subtle incense burning, and handmade ceramics lined the walls. All of the teas were stored in refrigerators and there was a menu that read like a wine list. There was such attention to every detail, all of which felt new and inspiring to me. I left that day intent on working there when I moved to New York. And a few months later, on December 31, 2007, I did move there from Boston. I went back to the store several times and bought every Japanese tea they had on the menu. I searched for the names of the places they came from—unsure how to pronounce Fukuoka or Kumamoto—and I did my best to remember their locations relative to Tokyo, the only city in Japan I knew of. I attempted to memorize the description of each tea and brewed each one carefully, figuring out my personal favorites along the way. A month later, I stopped by Ito En and asked if they were hiring. A clerk passed along the manager's card, and I sent an email that night. I waited. No reply. I sent another a week later. No reply. Ten days later I sent another. Finally, a response: "Please stop emailing. And we have an opening. Please come for an interview next Wednesday." I interviewed and was hired in February 2008.

On my first day of work, I showed up ten minutes early and waited outside the door on Madison Avenue. My boss came running down the street flustered. "TV Tokyo is coming to film this morning. I need you to sweep the store, mop, and then wait off to the side." As I finished mopping, the TV crew entered carrying cameras and gear. The talent was a comedy duo comprised of an American who spoke fluent Japanese and his counterpart, a Tokyo native. The crew huddled, and the director began pointing in my direction, while my boss nodded *no* emphatically, with a pained expression. After several minutes of this my boss approached me

and explained that the crew was doing a profile of the store for Japanese TV and wanted an American perspective on how Japanese tea was being sold and spoken about in the United States. Since my boss was Japanese she didn't fit the bill for the segment. "Sure, I said. Happy to help."

"Are you sure?" she asked, nervously, as it was my first day on the job. "Just keep your answers short and do your best to speak generally if you do not know something."

"Sure thing."

I set up behind the tea counter and got my bearings. The hosts would walk in to be greeted like customers and then ask me a few questions.

Action.

What happened next surprised even me. I greeted the talent, made small talk, and went on to answer every question they had in surprising detail.

"What is your favorite tea?" they asked.

"Right now I am enjoying this deep-steamed sencha from Makino-hara in Shizuoka. I think it has a wonderful balance and it's also a great value."

"Wow, Shizuoka. Even in Japan we know that is a famous place for tea."

"Right! It is the largest production area in Japan and chances are, if you are based in Tokyo, your tea is coming from there."

"This is a beautiful piece," one of the hosts said, pointing to a cast-iron kettle.

"This is our traditional kama, most famously used in the Japanese tea ceremony. These are made in Iwate Prefecture and enhance the flavor of the water."

And so on. In my excitement, the information just came flowing out. "Cut!"

We did it in one take. When I looked over, the whole crew and my boss were staring at me.

"Zach, are you an actor? How did you do that?" my boss asked.

"No. I'm a jazz drummer who loves Japanese tea," I replied.

Ever since that day I have been on a journey to go deeper, learn more, and spend as much time in the beautiful world of Japanese tea as I can.

After I had worked for two years at Ito En, the company made a decision to close the shop. I was called into an office, told the news, and given a severance check. I knew I wouldn't see a lump sum of money that large any time soon, and I decided to use the money to book a monthlong trip to Japan. I had friends from college now living in Japan who could

Left: Tea auction, Shizuoka Prefecture *Right:* Vintage kettle

help me get around, but more importantly I just knew I had to go. I was looking for tea.

My first encounter with the culture in Japan came immediately upon touchdown at Narita International Airport. As the plane taxied and parked at the gate, I looked out of the window and saw two baggage handlers look directly at the plane, bending into a deep, slow bow to the airplane and the guests aboard. They held it for about five seconds then slowly returned to standing. I could sense I was entering a new chapter in my life.

It wasn't long after I arrived that I had my first cup of tea. It is hard to express exactly how different the experience was compared to my prior experiences with tea. Having spent two years working at the premier Japanese tea shop in America, I had more experience drinking Japanese tea than most. And it was my understanding that the freshness of the product I had sold was first-class. I was wrong. The flavor of the tea in Japan can only be described as electrifying. It was like every cup of tea I had had up to that point was made up of two things: water and tea. The flavors of the tea and the water were present in an equilibrium. The first time I experienced tea in Japan, it was like the tea had fused with the water and penetrated it. The water was now just a sensation. The flavor of the tea was deep and profound, with an intoxicating aroma that was complete. The best way to describe this would be to compare it to a great soup, in which you sense the water as a texture and not a flavor. Well-made Japanese tea offers the same experience. A density and completeness that is almost always lacking in tea brewed in America. This was my first lesson. Tea in Japan had more flavor and aroma. Why?

Because it was fresher. In Japan, tea is processed and stored well. And because demand in the local market is high, tea is consumed quickly and does not sit on the shelves for long (of course there are exceptions; tea does go stale in Japan, but much less frequently than in America). The second lesson I learned is that water is incredibly important for making great tea. And the softness of most Japanese water is perfectly suited for it. In fact, Japanese teas are developed to best suit the local water. So it's no mistake that most Japanese teas taste great with Japanese soft water.

Left: The author packing tea in Fukuoka Prefecture
Right: Two generations of the Oota family, farmers from Ureshino, Saga Prefecture

DEVELOPING RELATIONSHIPS

When I started visiting Japan more frequently, and heading out to the countryside to meet producers, I wasn't aware of the norms of rural business. But I was lucky enough to have some friends from Fukuoka Prefecture who were able to clue me into the rhythms of life in the countryside. As we rattled up the hill into the mountains in eastern Fukuoka Prefecture, I started to see a world vastly different from Tokyo, Kyoto, and Fukuoka city. The areas where I traveled were all tea-producing regions and almost all supported rice production, forestry, and farming as well. The communities in these agricultural areas are tight-knit, and business is usually conducted between families that have known each other for generations. In a word, these communities are insular. But beyond that, agricultural business in Japan operates in a way that can seem counter-intuitive to westerners. Money and the sale of goods is not always the most important factor in a farming company's decision-making. The future and the continuation of the family business is key. Making a quick buck at the risk of losing control of the venture is universally avoided. So businesses in the countryside tend to grow slowly and deliberately, taking smaller risks. Of course innovation is important for any business to survive—but it is valued only in relation to a deliberate protection of other business matters. This, along with Japanese being the primary language of business and a typical unfamiliarity with foreigners, means most rural companies have no desire to work with companies outside of their established circle.

So I met with the growers, still a tourist but with a genuine interest in the business of tea. And I began to record proprietors' common concerns about developing their businesses beyond the borders of Japan: the language barrier, the incursion of Western business practices, and the complications of fax-based ordering and international payments. It became apparent that if I hoped to work directly with Japanese growers, these points would have to be addressed.

Having had the luck of meeting several warm and welcoming folks living in Fukuoka Prefecture, I started to wonder what it would look like if I could establish a company that was based in Japan and functioned more or less like a domestic trade partner with the producers. If I could have someone communicate our orders in Japanese, fax them through, receive the shipments locally, and pay by a Japanese bank, I thought it might alleviate the pressure on the tea makers, encouraging them to supply tea to me. Well, it almost worked. When I would propose the idea, I could sense a tinge of skepticism. I guess it sounded like such an outlandish idea that the growers didn't think I was serious. But good fortune was on my side, as I had befriended someone well known in the Japanese tea industry, a wholesaler of traditional Japanese tea wares, who drove me to the first farm, sat at the table, and vouched for me to the president. He

Left: The author with an award-winning gyokuro producer in Hoshinomura, Fukuoka Prefecture *Right:* Sharing a laugh in the tea factory with the Kettl team

said, "I believe he is worth working with…and this could be something good for your business down the road. Zach is serious and you should trust him." The door unlocked and they agreed, which opened the door for me to be able to work with other farms too. Thus began the beginnings of Kettl.

THE START

After setting up a small apartment that would function as our office, I began to order small amounts of tea to package and ship to New York. In my haste, I hardly thought about how I was going to sell the tea. I created a website, opened an Instagram account, and then…waited. After a week I realized more energy and creativity was going to be necessary to get a larger audience interested in Japanese tea. I decided I should market to restaurants. While I knew I was offering the best tea being made in Japan, I felt that a slogan like "Japan's best tea" was equivalent to "New York's best pizza." It sounds nice but carries very little weight. I knew that if chefs would stand behind our tea and serve it in their restaurants, our product would gain a following similar to that of the best wines of Europe or the finest produce of California.

My first account was almost too good to be true. I figured Japanese restaurants would be the most receptive to our tea, and I saw that chef David Bouley had just opened a flagship kaiseki restaurant in Tribeca, in partnership with the Tsuji Culinary Institute in Osaka. So I called. And after one ring a woman answered. I mentioned I had tea from Fukuoka and was curious if I might be able to set up a tasting. "The chef is from Fukuoka," she replied, "and he might be interested. Come tomorrow at 2 p.m." I couldn't believe it—I had my first meeting. David Bouley and the team loved the tea and placed an order. I had no tax ID number. No business bank account. Not even a business card. But I had the best Japanese tea in the United States, which I learned that day was the most important thing. Having top-quality product was all the mattered. I biked back to my apartment, and to the surprise of the restaurant's staff I returned the same day with the teas. Apparently, we also had same-day delivery. Another epiphany: service matters!

Our business spread by word of mouth, and a year on we were lucky enough to be supplying tea to some of the best chefs in New York City: Jean Georges, César Ramirez of Brooklyn Fare, Thomas Keller, and so on. Their passionate front-of-house teams talked about our teas to their guests, leaving an impression. Soon diners were finding us online and our retail business was born. And today we value the stories behind the products of our network of producers throughout Japan, because they are such an important part of the narrative. Our office in Japan has proved important, because keeping the tea fresh and fulfilling orders quickly allows Kettl to supply teas to the West that until now were not available outside of Japan's domestic market. It is my hope that this book can be another step in helping people discover the deep and rich world of Japanese tea. A world I have fallen in love with and a world I think many of you will love as well.

To discovering the beauty of Japanese tea: cheers!

Part One

THE REGIONS: FROM HISTORY TO HARVEST

———

CHAPTER ONE

Japanese Tea, a History

THE HISTORY OF TEA IN JAPAN IS RICH AND SPANS OVER ONE thousand years. Japanese tea developed alongside many of the country's most important historical events, such as its first encounters with China, the expansion of trade with the West, and developments in Japanese art and aesthetics. My interest in Japanese tea lead me to pursue a deeper understanding of its historical significance through oral interviews with tea historians and farmers in Japan. While by no means exhaustive, the timeline below provides key dates and events leading up to the present day.

HISTORY OF TEA IN JAPAN

Nara Period, Tang Dynasty (Eighth Century)
- Japan carries out diplomatic missions to Chang'an in China.

Heian Period, Tang Dynasty (794–1185)
- In 804, two Japanese monks, Kuukai and Saichou, are introduced to tea by Chinese monks in China and are the first in Japan's history to mention tea.

Koicha tea prepared during chanoyu, the traditional tea ceremony

- The very first tea seeds (*Camellia sinensis*) are planted by Saichou in Japan, in 805.
- The book *Kuikū kokushi* is the first reliable reference to tea: it lists 815 as the first mention of tea drinking in Japan and states that tea was served to Emperor Saga.
- At the emperor's request, tea is planted in and around Buddhist temples and consumed by monks. At this time, tea is not yet a drink of the people.

Kamakura Period (1185–1333)
- The Buddhist monk Eisai returns from China in 1191 and plants tea seeds on the island of Kyushu (Saga/Fukuoka).
- Seeds are given to the monk Myōe and planted at Kozan-ji in Toganoo outside Kyoto.
- In the year 1211 Eisai writes the *Kissa yōjōki (Drink tea and prolong life)*, the first text that outlines the specific health enhancing properties of tea. Eisai is most famous for offering tea as a hangover cure to the Emperor Monamoto no Sanetomo.

- As tea gains traction, tea betting games called tōcha become popular. During the games, contestants must distinguish honcha from hicha (true Toganoo or Uji tea from other teas). During this time karamono, or Chinese ceramics, are also very popular in Japan and are collected widely.

Muromachi Period (1336–1573)

- Shogun Ashikaga Yoshimasa builds the first shoin-style tearoom at Ginkakuji.
- The austerity of this new style of tearoom (chashitsu) is thought to have been a step toward the formal chanoyu tea ceremony that will emerge several hundred years later.
- It is said that Yoshimasa's tea master was Murata Shukō, also known as Murata Jukō. Shukō is credited with developing the muted "cold and withered" design language of the tea ceremony now often referred to as wabi sabi. He advocated combining imported Chinese wares with rough ceramics made in Japan in an effort to "harmonize Japanese and Chinese tastes." This intentional usage of simple or flawed utensils with a wabi (appreciation of the imperfect) aesthetic came to be referred to as wabi-cha. Shukō, however, did not embrace the idea of a fully wabi approach to chanoyu. By contrast, Takeno Jōō, who studied under one of Shukō's disciples, was dedicated to the elaboration of the wabi style in tea utensils as well as the decor of the tearoom.

Azuchi-Momoyama Period (1568–1600)

- Sen no Rikyū formalizes much of the traditional tea ceremony. Perhaps the most influential character in the history of Japanese tea, Rikyū served as tea master to both daimyos Oda Nobunaga and Toyotomi Hideyoshi.

Edo Period (1603–1867)

- Loose-leaf tea is introduced from China and popularized by the monk and poet Baisao.

A moment in the tearoom

- In 1738, Nagatani Soen develops a new process for drying and rolling tea leaves, thus inventing the style of tea that is now called sencha.
- Developments in tea production and the modernization of the tea industry with new technologies for farming and processing tea in Japan continue.

The history of tea in Japan is long and spans centuries, paralleling the development of art, religion, and culture through the many periods of Japan up through the present. Tea was first introduced to Japan during the Nara period (Tang dynasty in China), when diplomatic caravans traveled from Japan to the capital city of Chang'an, now present-day Xi'an in Shaanxi province. These diplomatic delegations were the first to encounter Chinese culture and its systems of government, religion, painting, and pottery. Tea too was introduced as a medicine said to clear the mind and body of the evils of sickness. Tea truly began to make its mark in Japan during the Heian period around the year 804, when after studying Buddhist meditation in China, the Japanese monks Kuukai and Saichou brought the very first tea seeds back to Japan. The lore goes that Saichou planted the first tea seeds in Kyushu—likely present day Saga Prefecture. According to the historical text *Kuikū kokushi*, Emperor Saga was first served tea in the year 815. He was a sinophile with a deep respect for Chinese poems; because of that he readily adopted tea and was its earliest major Japanese supporter. With the emperor's endorsement, the reputation of tea and its elixir-like effect continued spreading among Japanese monastics. At the urging of the emperor, tea seeds were propagated in and around Buddhist temples, and soon tea was being consumed by the monks. The famous story goes that the tea provided the monks with a steady stream of energy (in the form of caffeine and theanine) that kept them alert for their long overnight meditation sessions. Tea allowed them to find a suitable state of mind, opening them to a necessary awareness of their surroundings.

The next important chapter of Japan's tea history also involves a Buddhist monk introducing tea from China. In the year 1191 (the Kamakura period), the monk Eisai returned from China and began propagating tea in Kyushu. He also shared tea seeds with the monk Myōe at his temple Kozan-ji just outside of Kyoto in Toganoo. This moved tea

closer to Japan's cultural and governmental capital where it had a greater impact and experienced a new level of influence on the culture of the day. Tea was soon enjoyed by the literati and other cultured Kyotoites, which secured its fame not only as a medicine but also as a refined beverage of the cultured class. In 1211, Eisai would write the *Kissa yōjōki (Drink tea and prolong life)*, the first treatise on Japanese tea and a long-form love letter expressing the health benefits of the drink. While much of it was hyperbolic, and it espoused some dubious claims bordering on the magical, its impact was substantial. It was around this time that, according to legend, tea was introduced to the Emperor Monamoto no Sanetomo. After a night of heavy drinking he would be given tea to cure his hangover. By seeming to restore his vigor, tea gained the favor of Japan's most influential politician. With the support of the emperor and exposure in the refined upper class of Kyoto, tea became a deeply rooted fixture of Japanese culture.

As tea continued gaining popularity, it became the centerpiece of aristocratic culture. Tea became popularized through a wildly popular betting game called tōcha. During the game, contestants had to drink and distinguish between honcha, or "real tea," grown in Toganoo, and

hicha—tea grown outside of Toganoo. These games become raucous events with contestants winning and losing vast sums of money. At these gatherings the rich and cultured could also showcase their collections of karamono, handmade ceramics from China and Korea. The pieces were opulent representations of the contestants' wealth—and thus the art of ceramics became inseparable from the culture of tea.

It seems almost in direct response to these over-the-top displays of wealth and greed that a new form of "teaism" would be ushered in. And during the Muromachi period the shogun Ashikaga Yoshimasa built the foundation for this new movement in tea: the shoin tearoom at the temple Ginkakuji in Kyoto. Originally a place for monks to rest and socialize on breaks from meditation, the shoin room developed into the first space that resembled the well-known chashitsu, or tearooms, of contemporary chanoyu, the tea ceremony. It was Murata Shukō, the teacher of Yoshimasa, who then developed a new, more rustic style of tea reflective of Japan's Shinto past and its cultural respect for nature's rhythms, moving away from the classically opulent Chinese style. This new style became known as wabi-cha and celebrated the imperfect, muted, and withered.

Though all of these singular developments were significant, one person had a more direct and lasting impact on Japanese tea culture, and perhaps traditional Japanese culture in general, than anyone else: Sen no Rikyū. Rikyū was born in the town of Sakai in Osaka Prefecture. He studied tea from an early age and eventually became the student of the influential tea teacher Takeno Jōō, another early developer of the wabi-cha aesthetic. Rikyū studied to become a Buddhist monk, and later in life Zen thought would heavily influence his style of tea ceremony. Little is known of his life during its middle years; the period of Rikyū's greatest influence began in 1579, when at the age of fifty-eight he became the official tea master under Oda Nobunaga—a powerful daimyo and influential ruler. Working under Nobunaga, Rikyū enjoyed increasing fame, and his name was soon known throughout Japan. After Nobunaga's death, Rikyū began advising the powerful daimyo Toyotomi Hideyoshi. During this period, Rikyū feverishly developed many of the tenets of the tea ceremony that persist to this very day.

Rikyū carried on Murata Shukō's tradition of designing small, rustic tearooms that celebrated the shadows over the light, the withered over the new, and the nuances of the season. His most celebrated tearoom was Tai-an, a small two-tatami tearoom at Myouki-an, a temple on the outskirts of Kyoto and now one of Japan's national treasures. Rikyū was influential in developing many of the key architectural points of the tea-room. The nijiriguchi, or half-size door that serves as the entrance, was developed so that any who entered—whether a noble or a regular citizen—had to remove his sword and bend low. Once inside, all were equal.

Rikyū was also partly responsible for the development of the Raku tea bowls now famously used in the tea ceremony. He developed a relationship with the tile maker Raku Chojiro. Together they perfected the making of deep black rustic tea bowls. These bowls stood in stark contrast to the ornately decorated Chinese bowls that were in vogue at the time. Rikyū had a playful, artistic approach to the tea ceremony and created many tools that are now common today, including the bamboo chasen (tea whisk), chashaku (tea scoop), and hishaku (water ladle). Since the more rustic style of wabi tea seems common today, it may be hard to imagine just how radical Rikyū's developments were. But the mark of the master would go on to influence Japan well beyond tea—kaiseki, the famed long-form meal that today stands at the pinnacle of Japanese cuisine, was born in the tearoom. The flower-arranging method known as ikebana developed out of the tea ceremony as well.

Rikyū eventually fell out of favor with Hideyoshi. The daimyo accused Rikyū of being too independent, and in a flash of rage ordered him to commit seppuku, ritual suicide. Forced to oblige, Rikyū wrote the following poem before taking his own life:

> Welcome to thee,
> O sword of eternity!
> Through Buddha
> And through Daruma alike
> Thou hast cleft thy way

Japanese tea continued to develop, forever influenced by Rikyū.

Another highly influential person who profoundly shaped the world of Japanese tea was the Buddhist monk Baisao. Baisao was born in 1675 in the Hizen Province, today the Nagasaki and Saga Prefectures. Baisao became a Buddhist monk at an early age and traveled extensively, visiting temples and studying with Buddhist masters. At the age of forty-nine he left the monastic life quite abruptly and moved to Kyoto. He quickly became a local fixture and was befriended by well-to-do artists, philosophers, and the like. It was during this time that he became more deeply connected to tea, and around 1735 he began selling tea at different locations throughout Kyoto. While powdered and decocted teas were popular already, Baisao chose to sell sencha—a relatively new style of tea developed in Uji by Soen Nagatani (though it is thought that the tea was developed with the help of many others). Sencha was steamed, rolled, and dried, and then prepared for drinking by simmering in a tea kettle or brewing in a teapot. Baisao would continue to sell tea and write poems in Kyoto until he became disenchanted with what he saw as the stagnation of Japanese tea culture. As one of his final acts, Baisao burned his

A kama and hishaku ready to serve tea

most cherished tea tools in a fire as an act of open rebellion against the practice of attributing too much value to the old, revered brewing and drinking instruments. He died soon after.

Japan's tea industry continued to change during the nineteenth and twentieth centuries, with breakthroughs driven by Japan's equal commitments to traditional production and new technologies. Tea exports flourished during the Meiji and Shōwa periods (1868–1989) with up to twenty-thousand tons of tea being exported annually—most to the United States. After World War II, many steps in the process of making tea were mechanized, and the scale and sophistication of production and export grew exponentially. This allowed tea makers to not only make better tea, but also to make more of it. Ironically, while Japanese tea exports shrank in the postwar period due to higher global demand for coffee and cheaper teas from China and India, domestic demand increased.

Today some of the finest tea in the world is produced in Japan. And thanks to decades of technological innovations, Japanese tea makers can make exquisite tea at scale and keep it fresh using sophisticated packing and storing methods. And yet much of the traditional tea culture remains relatively unchanged. Japanese tea ceremonies today are practically the same as they would have been one hundred years ago. What has changed is the way tea is commonly enjoyed. Like coffee, tea is now enjoyed more as a lifestyle beverage both at home and in restaurants. Japanese bottled teas have become more sophisticated too, again due to postwar technology, and now make up the lion's share of domestic tea consumption.

In many ways, the future is bright for Japan's tea industry. As global demand for matcha continues to grow, even the skeptical industry leaders have begun to realize there is a market for Japanese tea beyond the nation's borders. And international appreciation for tea continues to grow as more quality tea makes its way west. Many foreign companies import tea from Japan to sell in their own countries, and with farmers and producers in Japan now on Instagram, a window into Japan's tea industry has begun to open. Japanese tea, I believe, is just getting started. Today, I think American understanding and appreciation of tea is on par with its appreciation of European wine in the 1970s. As more and more people experience fine, fresh tea, the demand will grow, and so will the industry around it. The fact that you are reading this book is proof of that!

So now the fun part—let's go deep and learn more about Japanese tea as it stands today.

Evaluating teas at auction in Shizuoka Prefecture

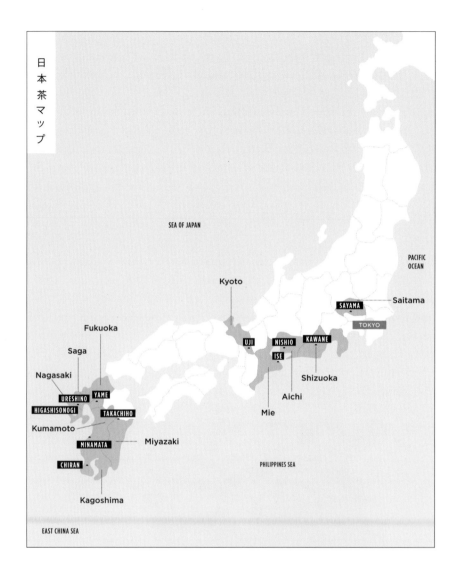

日本茶マップ

SEA OF JAPAN

PACIFIC OCEAN

Kyoto

SAYAMA ·········· Saitama

TOKYO

Fukuoka

Saga

UJI   NISHIO   KAWANE

Nagasaki

ISE

URESHINO   YAME

HIGASHISONOGI

Shizuoka

TAKACHIHO

Kumamoto

Aichi

MINAMATA   Miyazaki

Mie

CHIRAN

PHILIPPINES SEA

Kagoshima

EAST CHINA SEA

Main Tea Producing Regions of Japan

Japan is divided into prefectures, 11 of which produce most of our tea.

MAIN TEA PRODUCING PREFECTURES | ▲ TEA REGIONS | ▼ CAPITAL OF JAPAN

CHAPTER TWO

Notable Areas of Production

JAPAN PRODUCES TEA IN MANY OF ITS PREFECTURES, OR districts, and while the below does not cover every single one, those mentioned are important and worth familiarizing yourself with. Learning what you like to drink means understanding not only what style of tea you like, but also what area it comes from. Memorizing all the facts, figures, and locations can be hard work, so I suggest drinking a cup of tea from each prefecture you read about here. Tasting while learning always creates deeper connections!

SAYAMA, SAITAMA PREFECTURE

Sayama, just northwest of Tokyo, sits in Saitama Prefecture at the northern limit of the land used for commercial tea production in Japan. While lacking the name recognition of Shizuoka, Sayama supplies a good portion of the tea consumed in Japan's Kanto region. Sayama is well-known for its tea research institute and has been a leader in the experimentation on and propagation of dozens of cultivars native to the area. With a colder climate and higher chance of exposure to frost, this area necessarily hosts sturdier tea cultivars. Sayama is probably best known for producing fukamushi, or deep-steamed sencha. But some very distinctive

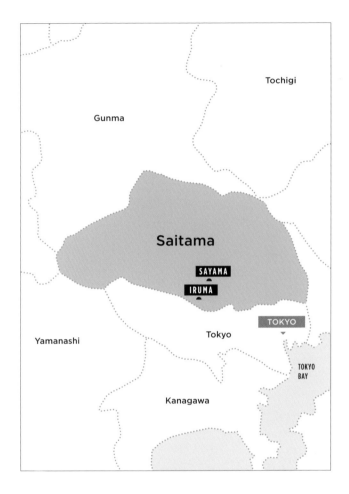

high-quality lighter-steamed teas as well as an array of unique pan-fired and slightly oxidized teas are being made in the Iruma area of the prefecture. Teas from Saitama tend to be refreshing, with lower levels of umami compared to teas found in other areas. A great place to start would be a sencha made from the namesake cultivar Sayama Kaori, or "Fragrance of Sayama."

SHIZUOKA PREFECTURE

Shizuoka Prefecture is Japan's "fertile crescent" of tea. And more specifically it's the mecca of sencha. Shizuoka boasts the most farms, the most land area dedicated to tea production, and the highest annual output of tea in the entire country. Without oversimplifying, Shizuoka can be divided into two camps: the deeper-steamed teas of the lowland towns such as Makinohara and Kakegawa, and the light-steamed senchas of the mountain areas of Kawane, Tenryū, Umegashima, and so forth.

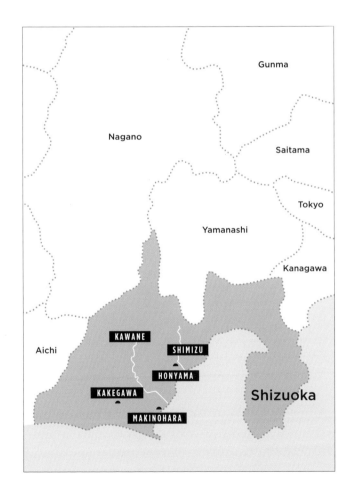

Shizuoka produces both tea in high-volume for mass consumption and some of the most coveted single-cultivar senchas available. One thing is for sure, it is a big place, and there is always more to discover. Try a fun taste comparison: A fukamushi sencha from Kakegawa and a light-steamed sencha from Kawane or Shimizu. You might be surprised how big a world sencha can be.

UJI, KYOTO PREFECTURE

Uji is the cultural home of Japanese tea. To this day, Uji remains the most historically significant location for tea production and culture in all of Japan. Matcha, gyokuro, and sencha were all developed in and around Uji. Today, Uji remains a commercial powerhouse and Uji tea has become a brand name the world over. Many families producing tea here have been doing so for hundreds of years. A mecca for the more refined teas like matcha and gyokuro, Uji produces teas that command some of the highest prices—a testament to its farmers' high level quality of production and the region's brand-name strength. Uji also continues to be a tea tourism hub as it is easily accessible from Kyoto by train.

FUKUOKA PREFECTURE

Fukuoka has the reputation of an up-and-coming prefecture that produces all styles of tea, most famously a traditional Dentou Hon Gyokuro. Fukuoka has taken the torch from Uji, and is now known as the region with the highest-quality gyokuro production. Additionally, matcha, sencha, and various commercially oriented teas are produced here as well, cementing its status as a growing commercial hub for tea. Fukuoka's strength lies in its favorable weather and strong local tea industry. With support from the local government, Fukuoka has climbed the ladder to become one of the regions with the most sought-after Japanese tea.

KAGOSHIMA PREFECTURE

Kagoshima is the second-largest of all tea-producing prefectures in Japan and will take the crown from Shizuoka to become the largest in the next few years. Kagoshima has a long history producing tea. Originally

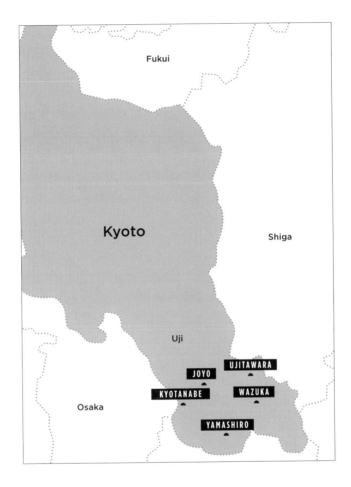

an area focused on black tea for overseas trade, Kagoshima has recently become a central area for sencha production. With its location in the south of Kyushu, Kagoshima benefits from having the earliest harvest of all tea regions in Japan. Producers here have had great luck grabbing a big piece of the market during the early-spring shincha season. Matcha and gyokuro production has picked up here, and with global demand for both rising, more unique varieties can be expected to emerge in the coming years.

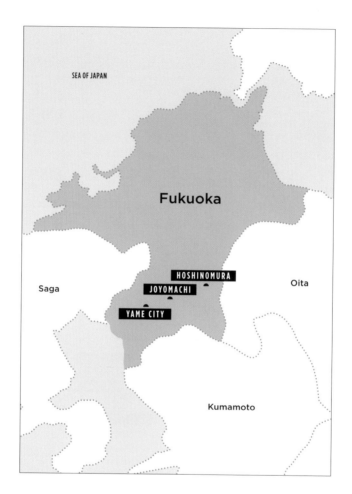

URESHINO, SAGA PREFECTURE

Ureshino is a small area on the western coast of Kyushu. Ureshino continues to primarily produce kamairicha, or pan-fired tea. Pan-firing was introduced from China and has been replaced with steaming in almost every other prefecture. Ureshino teas are focused and fresh, and often utilize unique cultivars. Getting to know tea from this area is a wonderful way to experience another side of Japanese tea.

MIE PREFECTURE

While it is the third-largest area of tea production in Japan, Mie has little of the brand recognition of Shizuoka or Kagoshima. It so happens that the area around Ise is famous for producing both fukamushi- and kabuse-style sencha. The bulk of these teas are sold to be blended and often make their way to the tea markets of Shizuoka and Kagoshima. There are several smaller producers who grow and manufacture 100 percent unblended "Ise cha," but this tea is almost impossible to find. We hope to see more of it in the future.

KUMAMOTO AND MIYAZAKI PREFECTURES

Both Kumamoto and Miyazaki Prefectures are located in the southern quadrant of Kyushu and produce kamairicha, orthodox sencha, and black tea. Both prefectures are also gaining a reputation for their commitment to organic farming methods. Look here for more unconventional teas.

Tea fields in Yame, Fukuoka Prefecture

CHAPTER THREE

Growing Tea in Japan

WHILE JAPAN IS A SMALL COUNTRY, ROUGHLY TWENTY-TWO OF its forty-seven prefectures produce tea of some kind. Japan is home to a variety of microclimates and soil types. That in combination with the country's many unique regional production methodologies means Japan produces teas with distinct regional characteristics. Unlike Indian teas, which are harvested in multiple seasons, Japanese tea is mainly harvested in the spring. Although the work of harvesting is compressed into one quarter of the calendar year, growing tea is a yearlong pursuit—and during the harvest season many important choices have to be made weekly, daily, and sometimes by the hour.

A NEW SEASON

Japan's tea-growing season officially begins when the tea plants awaken from their winter dormancy in mid-to-late February. The plants grow slowly through the cold temperatures of February and March, and the new spring tea buds begin to appear in early April. Tea harvesting begins at that time in the south of Japan and steadily moves northward with most of the first harvest taking place by mid-May. The exception is at higher elevations, where the cooler weather means a *(continued on p. 48)*

SHINYA
YAMAGUCHI

Perhaps no one understands the impacts of soil, terroir, and manufacturing on tea better than Shinya Yamaguchi. Yamaguchi-san's intense passion and incredible attention to detail are legendary. He is regarded as an expert not only in the production of tea, but as a master sommelier in evaluating the quality of tea as well. He is one of only ten people in the Japanese tea industry to have a perfect jūdan rating—meaning he has perfect scores when it comes to tea evaluation. Other producers refer to him with accolades like "genius," "legend," and "once in a generation," among others. Yamaguchi-san and his family have been growing tea in the small town of Hoshinomura—central Fukuoka—since World War II. The soil, mountain air, and fresh streams make it an ideal location, but the community and its commitment to one another is also bedrock to the success of this tiny town that produces Japan's top-rated gyokuro.

Zach Mangan: You belong to a generation of tea farmers. Can you share with us a little bit of the history of your business?

Shinya Yamaguchi: My family started as tea farmers after World War II. Back then, everyone was growing tea in their backyard. My grandfather convinced the local tea farmers around Hoshinomura village to share their tea. That was the origin of our business. He then started finishing tea and creating shiagecha [refined or finished tea]. Currently we have a factory, warehouse, and refrigeration. The building we are currently in was built in 1978, and our new factory was built in 1999. So, we don't have a long history.

How has your business evolved over time?

We are now a tea manufacturer, so we mainly focus on the finishing, or processing aracha into shiagecha. But since we own our farm, we are able to produce many types of products. We also do packaging, wholesaling, and retailing.

What are your responsibilities within your business?

I am the senior managing director, so I decide the strategy of the company. But personally, I still prefer a hands-on approach and making tea. So, while I play a big role in setting the direction for the business, I also do cultivar testing and analysis in my own farm. I like to explore the tea's possibilities. It is my passion.

When I talk to farmers in Uji, I have noticed that they like keeping tradition and history. However, in your case, it seems you are very open to trying something new. Is this a characteristic of Kyushu, or is it specific to your family?

I'm not sure, but I think it's both. After finishing my tea studies in Shizuoka and Kyoto, I started to notice the good things about my hometown, such as the soil quality, the altitude, and of course the people. But I don't think we have yet realized Yame's full potential. And that is exactly what motivates me to challenge many things.

If you think about it, Uji tea sells no matter what since it has a long tradition [Uji has major regional recognition, similar to Burgundy or Bordeaux in French wine]. But since we don't have such history, we need to compete on quality or new ideas that can help us to stand out. And that drive to produce high-quality tea is the reason why we have been able to continue receiving Daijin awards.

How important do you think soil is to the flavor of the tea?

I think that soil quality is more important than the farmer's techniques. When you look at all areas that produce tea in Japan, even

So, is the soil what determines the quality of the tea?
Generally speaking, yes. However, there are some cultivars, such as Okumidori, Tsuyuhikari, and Saemidori, that can be grown steadily regardless of the soil quality. There is always a way to make delicious tea even if the soil is not great.

if the weather is similar, and they have the same temperature and the same amount of rain, the production regions of so-called special-grade or high-grade teas are very limited. And that is because of the different soil quality.

What is your desert-island tea?
That is a difficult question, but I think I would bring matcha.

later harvest around late May or early June, depending on the season's weather. The first harvest and release of the year is referred to as shincha (*shin* means new, *cha* means tea). Shincha is an indicator of the arrival of spring and this young, fresh green tea is sold for only a small window of time—roughly a month. This new release can be likened to Beaujolais nouveau wine—a celebration of the arrival of spring and a look at what is coming for the year ahead.

A CHANCE THAT ONLY COMES ONCE A YEAR

Growing tea is an art. And the best producers view it as a cherished opportunity. Think of it this way: a farmer who works for fifty years will only get a chance to create fifty harvests of tea. Imagine a baker that must perfect a loaf of sourdough in just fifty tries! So, each year farmers must use all of their past experiences to shape their current crop of tea. There are countless things to consider. For example, a farmer must know what cultivars will do well in her field. The Saemidori cultivar flourishes in the hot spring months of Kyushu in the south of Japan but is too sensitive to frost exposure to be grown in Saitama in the north. Conversely, the hearty Yamakai cultivar is at home in the cool mountains of Shizuoka but would wither in the heat of Nagasaki. If this reminds you of wine, you're on the right track. Tea cultivars are in many ways analogous to the grape varietals used in winemaking. And as with wine, the land on which the tea is grown can have a momentous impact on flavor and aroma. The combination of microclimate and soil composition, the way the field is managed, and other choices by the farmer create the terroir of each tea—the "taste of the place." Choices made on the smallest scale have a big impact: Should the grower wait to harvest on Wednesday when it will rain but the leaves will be at their prime, or harvest two days before when the weather is more pleasant? How much of a difference will that two-day window make? Is there a right answer? Many such questions and their answers inform the almost mystical nature of tea cultivation.

Tea fields in Honyama, Shizuoka Prefecture

WINTER WORK: PREPARING THE SOIL, PREPARING THE MIND

While the winter months could be considered the off-season for tea farmers, there is in fact plenty of work to do. Preparation for the year's tea begins with field management. The tea bushes are generally cut back in the fall and grow back slowly over the winter, during which time they require some maintenance. While the tea bushes appear inactive during the short days and cold nights of winter, they are actually in the process of storing energy. It is during this time that the soil must be cared for, and nutrients, through fertilizer, are applied to the soil around the tea bushes. The tea plants slowly absorb these nutrients and begin using them to push forth the small, tender leaves of the spring harvest. Understanding the relationship between soil and the tea plants' nutritional needs is paramount to producing great tea. In my experience, the tea producers with the deepest sensitivity to their tea plants invariably become obsessed with the health of their soil. As the farmer Shinya Yamaguchi puts it: "Soil is more important than a farmer's technique." So, it makes sense that an obsession with soil would lead to the most delicious tea—tea with true personality.

In addition to field management, tools and machinery used for producing tea are serviced and repaired during the winter. The factory is cleaned. The tea fields are surveyed and any new tea saplings that may

Tezumi, or hand-harvesting, Shizuoka Prefecture

be planted in the spring are nurtured in the greenhouse. Additionally, the winter is a time to consider hopes and goals for the upcoming season. Because once the spring growing cycle is upon them, farmers have little time to think—it is a crushing cycle of near around the clock work.

THE SPRING HARVEST

The harvest season begins in the south of Japan and slowly moves northward spanning the period from early April in the southern islands up through mid-to-late May for the northern areas of Japan and those places at higher elevation. The tea bush is a perennial evergreen, *Camellia sinensis*, and each year small spring buds appear on the top of the bush. These young, tender leaves are what is used for the highest-quality teas. Depending on the farm, the tea leaves can be either hand-picked or machine harvested. The most delicate teas are hand-harvested in a process called tezumi, in which a skilled tea picker will navigate the tea fields with a collection basket and quickly pick the young fresh leaves, known as shinme. Less than 5 percent of tea in Japan is hand-harvested. The stamina, visual acuity, and nimble fingers involved in hand harvesting make it very difficult and specialized work. Most often, women over the age of seventy are employed in tezumi, and the same group of ladies will work year after year for a farmer or group of farmers with whom they form lasting friendships.

Harvesting tea on the slopes of Honyama in Shizuoka

The majority of tea is machine harvested. Depending on the size of the farm, these harvesters can range in size from something akin to a large Weedwacker to a drivable vehicle similar to a small corn combine. Machine shearing does the job faster but inevitably cuts more mature leaves and stems that will have to be separated out later. While the highest-quality sencha is surely hand-harvested, many delicious and high-quality teas are made with machine-harvested leaves. Once the tea leaves are harvested, the farmer engages in a race against time. Tea leaves, once picked, begin to oxidize. Green teas such as sencha must be processed before that happens.

ARACHA: PROCESSING TEA THE JAPANESE WAY

Although each region of Japan has its own unique method for creating delicious tea, these have more similarities than differences. And they all share one thing: the aracha process.

Aracha can be loosely translated to "crude tea." Aracha is produced by a special method developed in Japan that turns fresh tea leaf into stable, storable green tea. What makes it so unique? A small producer in China, for example, might harvest the leaves, heat them, and shape them to create the finished product. That product will not undergo any further processing or blending—the tea is now completely finished and could begin to suffer the adverse effects of light, heat, and moisture—all enemies of green tea's subtle flavors and aromas. Tea that undergoes the aracha process, on the other hand, is shelf stable and storable, giving resellers and manufacturers choices for how to blend or process the final product. In short, aracha is a uniquely Japanese way of processing tea leaf.

ARACHA: CRUDE TEA

Steaming

The most important step in the aracha process is the swift application of heat, in the form of steam, to the freshly harvested leaves. Heat works to deactivate the enzymes that would cause the tea to break down and begin to oxidize. What exactly is oxidation? The most common example used to explain it is the browning of an apple: Once you slice an apple and the inner flesh is exposed to air, it begins to brown almost immediately.

Tea leaves undergoing deep steaming, Kagoshima

This browning process is oxidation. When the tea leaf is picked, its inner cellular tissue is exposed to air, and this triggers the production of the enzyme polyphenol oxidase (PPO). PPO oxidizes the polyphenols in the tea and creates a new set of chemicals known as quinones. The quinones react with amino acids in the tea leaf (or apple) and begin to produce melanins, which are responsible for that brown color. Green tea is steamed to prevent any oxidation, while other styles of tea, like oolong and black tea, are allowed to undergo varying degrees of oxidation. This accounts for the red, brown, or even black color of their leaves.

The Rolling Dryer

After steaming, a great deal of moisture is present both inside leaves and on their surfaces. So, a machine called a rolling dryer uses both pressure and hot air to lower the leaves' moisture content. The machine is shaped like a drum and tumble dries the tea leaves with hot air and large metal paddles that replicate the way a human hand would gently knead the leaves.

Primary Rolling

The primary rolling process involves a machine that spins in a clockwise motion and applies pressure, tying the tea leaves into small knots while further reducing moisture. During this process the cell walls of the leaves begin to break down, making the product more pliable and releasing aromatic compounds. By this point, a skilled producer will have a very good idea of what the profile of the finished tea will be just by the scent of the leaf.

Secondary Rolling

The secondary rolling process continues the work of applying heat and lowering the moisture content of the leaves, while also untangling the small knots and giving shape to the leaf. This step transforms the leaves into something visibly recognizable as tea. After this step, the moisture content of the tea will sit between 12 and 15 percent, and the tea leaves will begin to take on the familiar needle shape of sencha.

Top: Evaluation by sight *Middle:* Fresh steamed tea leaves
Bottom: Evaluation by tasting

Final Rolling

The final rolling process involves very high pressure and more heat. This shaping stage is important, and a job well done is often a point of pride for a producer. The length of the initial steaming directly impacts the final shape of the leaf. Lighter-steamed teas known as asamushi remain much more needle-like after the final rolling, while deep-steamed fukamushi teas appear to be broken in smaller pieces.

Final Drying

After final rolling, the tea undergoes a final drying to lower the moisture content of the leaf to about 5 percent. This crude tea is then bagged into sixty-six-pound (thirty kilogram) airtight bags and cold stored to protect it from light, heat, and moisture. It will later be selected for blending at market, where a tea reseller might buy two different lots of aracha based on their flavor profile and blend them to create a desired outcome.

SHIAGECHA: FINISHED TEA

Shiagecha refers to aracha that has been blended and finished—a refined leaf suitable for sale. The shiagecha finishing process both lowers the final moisture level in the leaf to around 2 percent and removes any stems or coarse leaves, leaving only leaves of a uniform size and shape. Also, of great importance in the shiagecha process is the final firing of the leaf. This step is called hiire and can be thought of as a gentle baking. The heat caramelizes some of the sugars in the leaves, imparting a soft sweetness and a rich aroma. After this process the tea leaves can be packaged and made ready for sale.

FRESH TEA YEAR-ROUND

These distinctly Japanese processes make it possible to drink fresh, vibrant tea year-round. Kettl customers often ask, "Why does your tea taste so fresh compared to what I usually buy?" The answer is this: instead of buying all of our tea once a year, we order our teas weekly. Upon ordering, our suppliers process aracha into the shiagecha that we sell to our customers. This made-to-order system is unique to Japan and accounts for the freshness of high-quality Japanese teas, imbuing them with a "just-harvested" aroma and a tantalizing depth of flavor.

To sum up everything you've just read, there are many key factors that impact the final flavor profile of a given Japanese tea. Japanese tea starts with a farmer's understanding of the local climate and soil, which influences everything from the cultivars he grows to how and when he harvests. Next, decisions made at the aracha factory have a huge impact on a given tea's flavor. Lastly, decisions are made during shiagecha processing that determine the flavor balance of the final product. At every step there countless choices to make, all of which are represented in your teacup.

Tea fields, Honyama region in Shizuoka Prefecture

Part Two

THE

GROWERS

AND

THEIR

TEAS

—

CHAPTER FOUR

Sencha

SENCHA REFERS TO THE LARGEST CATEGORY OF GREEN TEAS produced in Japan. Most simply, sencha is made from tea leaves that have been harvested, steamed, and then processed into aracha, or crude tea, and finally finished into shiagecha (See pages 52–57). Sencha is made in almost every tea-producing area in Japan from as far north as Saitama Prefecture to as far south as the southern island of Tanegashima. Sencha truly encompasses a world of stylistic differences and flavor profiles with each region producing teas that highlight its many different qualities. Because of the sheer volume of sencha produced in Japan there are endless variations to discover, as with the red wines of France or the whiskeys of Scotland. Simply put, of all the types of Japanese tea, sencha probably boasts the widest range of styles.

GROWING AND PRODUCTION

With so much variety among senchas, it is paramount that those who farm it understand the complexities of local weather and soil, and know which cultivars will do well in their fields. For example, a farmer must be tuned into which cultivars will be ready at what times so they can create a harvest schedule and not be overwhelmed on any *(continued on p. 66)*

JIRO
KATAHIRA

Jiro Katahira is a celebrated sencha farmer based in Shizuoka, Japan. Following in his father's footsteps, Katahira-san is now responsible for his family's farm, which produces more than twenty varieties of single-cultivar sencha. His reputation for excellence has earned him awards and the respect of the industry. Katahira-san is considered an expert in the field of single-cultivar sencha.

Zach Mangan: Can you tell us a bit about your family history?

Jiro Katahira: Well, our tea business was started by my grandfather, Isamu. At that time the business was very seasonal: tea in the spring and farming oranges and cutting lumber in the winter. When my father took over, we quit growing oranges. And we were doing both tea-making and lumbering alternatively in summer and winter. When I joined, I was making tea in the spring and summer and cutting lumber in the winter. Now we are focused only on tea.

Why do you think Shizuoka developed as the epicenter of green tea production in Japan?

Shizuoka has a history of making tea—but it is not really that much longer than that of the other regions of Japan. And of course, we have pristine land and unique conditions for growing green tea. But personally, more than both things, I believe that the personality of the people in Shizuoka is what led to it becoming such a renowned region. The mentality of one guy saying, "I can do it better!" and another guy saying "No, I can do it better" really pushed us all to grow and create high-quality tea. I think that is the most important characteristic of Shizuoka.

Can you describe what is so unique about high mountain sencha, like what you make?

The differences in taste of different areas are impacted by both agricultural factors and also the regional preference for taste. For example, the soy sauce in Kyushu is sweeter, right? That's because people in Kyushu *want* umami. So, it can be produced that way. Much of Japan, including parts of Shizuoka, want more umami in regard to tea as well, and that can be achieved quite easily by shading the plants. But I would say the unique qualities—the freshness and fragrance—of Shizuoka tea cannot be replicated so easily and therefore are unique to this area.

And what do you think accounts for this unique fragrance?

First, I would probably say it's from the soil. Second, the fact that we steam our teas so lightly helps to maintain the unique fragrance of the area. Nationally, much of the tea is deep-steamed and I think it can be harder to distinguish the area. Of course, our unique cultivars are a big part of our teas as well. We are also very restrained in our use of fertilizer, and this leaves room for the flavor of the soil to be more at the forefront. I am not speaking against these other practices—it is just our way and what makes this area unique. Recently, much of Shizuoka has begun making fukamushi (deep-steamed) tea to suit national tastes. But I still feel committed to making tea this way, even if it is a very small amount in comparison to what is sold nationally.

You are known for your commitment to single cultivars. How many do you grow?

Currently twenty-six, of which twenty-two are mature enough to be harvested and drank.

And what should someone look for when trying to distinguish good-quality sencha?

Of course, there are many things to consider, but just learn to see the leaf quality. A dark, shiny leaf is important. The sheen on the leaf is a sign of the quality. There is a saying that you can see yourself reflected in the leaf of the highest-quality sencha. True or not, a good sheen is important!

And what is your preferred way to brew your sencha?

I usually use about 100 to 120 milliliters of water at sixty degrees Celsius with eight grams of leaf and brew for about a minute. This is a great starting place for our tea. Please note in order to brew this style you must use very soft, clean water.

What is your desert-island tea?

Well, that's the tea we made for hinpyoukai [the national tea fair] about thirteen years ago. That's because I've started to roll tea for hinpyoukai since then. My father stopped rolling and I started rolling. When I was cleaning the refrigerator, I found the tea my father rolled for hinpyoukai. That's what I want to drink. I'm keeping it with good care even now. I mean to drink it after my father passes away.

SENCHA

FLAVOR PROFILE:
Grassy, refreshing, and mildly sweet. The brewed tea has a rich neon green to highlighter-yellow color

ESTABLISHED PRODUCTION AREAS INCLUDE:
Shizuoka Prefecture: Kawane, Honyama, Shimizu, Kakegawa, and Makinohara
Fukuoka Prefecture: Yame
Kyoto Prefecture: Uji, Wazuka
Kagoshima Prefecture: Chiran, Kirishima

EMERGING PRODUCTION AREAS INCLUDE:
Saitama Prefecture, Gifu Prefecture

Left: Tetsuro Tsuchida, Kawane, Shizuoka Prefecture

particular day. Or, when it comes to soil, a farmer's field may be naturally deficient in one nutrient and have too much of another, requiring careful management of the land. It is this combination of weather, cultivar, and soil, along with the choices of the farmer, that creates the fascinating terroir of Japanese sencha.

Precisely because of these factors, sencha is really a myriad of styles and flavors as opposed to one fixed style of tea. Even within a single prefecture, micro-regional manufacturing styles exist. For example, in Shizuoka Prefecture alone, buying sencha can mean getting completely different teas, depending on where you are shopping: Light-steamed single-cultivar sencha from Kawane, deep-steamed blended sencha from Kakegawa, or medium-steamed, curled-leaf guricha-style sencha from the Izu peninsula.

Sencha's strength is that there are so many versions to choose from and learn about. Whether you like a golden brew that's lightly floral, a deep-green cup brimming with umami, or a nutty and layered tea perfect after a meal, you can find what you're after in the world of sencha. As you learn to enjoy sencha, it begins to reveal itself like an onion—layer upon layer of nuance with endless styles to try. When I hear someone say "I don't like sencha," it actually excites me, for there is surely a version of sencha out there for everyone. The key to sencha is to try as many styles as possible from as many regions as you can.

SOIL AND FERTILIZATION

The majority of Japan's major tea-growing regions lie south of Tokyo, and all lie within the country's humid subtropical zones, characterized by their hot, humid summers and cold-to-mild winters. Within the areas of production, topography and soil makeup are varied. While soil composition can vary within a single area, generally speaking *Camellia sinensis* requires soil that can drain quickly and is free of large rocks and debris. What separates good soil from great soil has a lot to do with chemical composition. The tea plant needs a combination of nutrients to thrive including nitrogen, potassium, and phosphorus. But much of these chemicals can be added to the soil by way of fertilization. The most common form of fertilizer for sencha is soy bean solids. Animal manure, fish meal, and other plant sources are also used. The schedule for applying fertilizers is not fixed, but most farmers will add it three to six times a year. The best teas always reflect a healthy, dynamic soil, and the best growers are the ones that have honed a sensitivity for the land on which they grow. I see it time and time again—the producers who are attuned to the land always get the best from it.

A family tea garden in Uji

A NOTE ON PESTS

In a tea field, the leaves of the tea plant are full of nutrients and abundant. A perfect target for insects. Farmers are inevitably faced with a choice of how to manage pests in the field. Depending on the location of the farm and the grower's personal approach, there are two main ways to manage pests: agricultural chemicals and natural pesticides. A farmer can also refrain from treating crops at all—a third option.

Japan has strict restrictions on pesticide use, but the fact is, pesticides are used. In most cases they are applied to the base of the plant, not the leaves, and there are strict cutoff dates for when a farmer must stop using them prior to harvest. While it is true that chemicals are used, intelligent use means very few teas in the Japanese marketplace show any chemical residue in third-party testing.

Natural insecticides vary in both style and effectiveness but are becoming more and more common. One approach is the use of sugar sprays to lure insects away from leaves. Another is the growing of cultivars with higher levels of catechin and caffeine, which naturally dissuade insects from eating the plants.

Lastly, location plays an important role in pest management. Teas grown higher up in the mountains see less pest activity than those grown in the flatlands. The cooler weather and less abundant vegetation mean fewer predators for the tea plants.

I am often asked about organic practices, and while I support organic farming wholeheartedly, it is important to realize teas stamped with "organic" are not necessarily well made or delicious. Like most things, tea production is not a black-and-white endeavor. The best teas come from the best growers who understand the complexity of nature. They work hard to find the balance between supporting what works in nature and using technology to improve what doesn't.

THE SENCHA FIELD

If you have seen tea fields in Japan—perhaps from the window of a speeding shinkansen, or bullet train—you have most certainly seen sencha. The rows of emerald hedges poised on the mountainsides, along with terraced rice paddies, make for some of the most idyllic views in rural Japan. While these sencha bushes are manicured to appear as a single hedge, they are in fact a network of small tea saplings that have grown close together, with each individual sapling fusing to create the appearance of one long row. While the height of the bush is fairly standard (about hip height), the width can vary depending on how the tea bushes will be harvested—either by hand or machine. Depending on the cultivar of the bush, its overall shape—as well as the shape of the leaf—will differ. But through uniform pruning, the bushes can be hard to tell apart. A healthy sencha bush will contain waxy, dark-green leaves from which the tender buds of the new crop will sprout in spring. The roots of sencha bushes do well in nutrient-dense, well-draining soil. Soil accounts for a large percentage of the personality of a sencha. Even within a small area, teas can vary quite drastically. Certain hills in small towns in Shizuoka are famous for the unique flavor they impart, and tea grown on them may fetch one and a half to two times more than the tea from across the road. Fertilizing, pruning, and general maintenance of the field also impact the ultimate quality of a tea.

Calculating buying price by abacus, Shizuoka tea auction

THE TEA MARKET

Much of the sencha that is grown in Japan doesn't necessarily move from the field directly to retail shelves. In fact, the majority of Japan's teas circulate within the prefectural tea markets. For example, the teas of Shizuoka will be bought and sold within Shizuoka's central tea market, and the teas of Kagoshima will be bought and sold within Kagoshima's central tea market, and so on. With some exceptions, of course. Generally, the tea leaf from each farmer is processed into aracha and then displayed alongside hundreds of others, side by side on black metal trays. A card accompanying each tea will display information about it including the cultivar, the harvest date, specific place it was grown, the farmer's name, and the amount available for purchase. The whole system is run by the prefectural tea board. Within the market there are three main groups: farmers (or their designated representatives), tea resellers who are there to bid on the teas, and representatives of the tea board. Both farmers and tea sellers must be registered in order to participate in the auction.

While many large-scale tea resellers have their own farms, most need more tea than they can grow to satisfy their customers' demand. The market serves as a way of connecting farmers who do not process their own tea with tea manufacturers who are in need of more product. The tea market is a small world, and most farmers and wholesalers know each other—so often deals are struck directly between farmers and resellers.

But the inspection of tea is important and requires a high level of skill and experience.

To the average person, or even someone well versed in tea, batches of tea leaves can look indistinguishable from one another. But each lot is unique and there are many telltale signs that let buyers know if the tea in front of them is one they should buy.

How can they tell? With the teas lined up, farmers and resellers will inspect the teas very carefully. First the teas will be judged visually. Each tea can be graded by the dry leaf's color and color consistency, shape, and gloss level. One of the most important ways of identifying quality is by handling the dry leaf. A great deal of information can be gleaned just by touching the tea. A seasoned expert can infer the moisture level, quality of processing, and overall caliber of a tea simply by rubbing it between his fingers. Next, the tea is lifted to the nose. Fragrance provides an incredible amount of information to a tea professional: steaming level, quality of picking, whether the tea was shaded, and much more. Once a tea is being seriously considered for purchase, five grams of it is added to a cup and steeped for five minutes in roughly one hundred milliliters of boiling-hot water. You might think that would scorch the tea

A family farm in Ureshino, Saga Prefecture

leaf—and you would be correct for thinking so. But this process allows all of the tea's components to steep out: the good and, more importantly, the bad. Tea professionals learn just as much from a tea's defects as from its strengths. Once the tea is brewed it is again evaluated, first visually and then by smell and taste. At this point most professionals have all the information they need to decide if they will bid on the tea. During the bidding process, farmers or their representatives deal directly with resellers in a process supported by the tea board. Deals happen fast, and hundreds of thousands of dollars of tea is bought and sold in a morning at the market. Once bidding is complete, teas are collected and transported to refrigerated storage before being blended and finished.

BLENDED SENCHA

Most typically, sencha is blended. Blending affords a tea producer both consistency and scale. As mentioned, many tea resellers grow a portion of their own tea. But Japan's strict land-use laws make it difficult for any one company to own vast amounts of land. To illustrate this point: most of the large tea fields you see in Shizuoka look like one large plantation but are in fact subdivided into zigzagging cross sections that belong to multiple owners. To grow a reselling business, more tea than what is available to one farmer is needed. Additionally, tea is an agricultural product and, like wine, will change year over year. Customers often come to expect a certain flavor or profile from a tea brand, and for a farmer to rely on one cultivar each year to produce that flavor is not realistic. Weather, changes in soil conditions, and manufacturing difficulties mean a tea producer cannot guarantee that one year's tea will taste like another. To mitigate this, blending is the norm. A chashi, or tea blender, is tasked with creating the "cuvée" blends that represent a company. To do this, the chashi blends the teas that are carefully selected at auction each year in different ratios to reproduce the established flavor of the company's products. It is hard to overstate the expertise required to faithfully match flavors by blending. And remember: chashi must make split-second decisions at the tea auction. Misreading the leaves can lead to a company ending up with a literal ton of tea that can't be used.

Teas are blended in the aracha state and then processed into shiage-cha. Sencha made from blends can be incredibly delicious. They often have a wonderful, layered harmony. I think of the chashi as building the teas like a pianist builds a chord on a piano: stacking flavors like notes to create a splendid harmony of flavor. Oftentimes, a bit of the previous year's tea is also blended in to maintain consistency. And the most incredible part is that if the chashi is doing his job, you would never know the difference.

In recent years, as farmers have stepped into the spotlight, the public's desire to experience the unique flavor of each individual cultivar has increased. And along with that consumers are now welcoming each year's subtle differences and eccentricities. That leads us to a newer phenomenon: single-cultivar sencha.

UNBLENDED SINGLE-CULTIVAR SENCHA

Blending is the traditional way that tea has been prepared for sale for years. The farmer grows tea and makes aracha and takes it to the marketplace where it is sold at auction. A reseller buys the tea and then a chashi blends it and it undergoes final processing. In the end, customers are treated to a standardized offering.

Somewhat recently, farmers have begun to grow their tea and process it all themselves in an unblended state—meaning the finished tea is 100 percent single-cultivar. Every leaf in your cup hails from the same garden. These teas are like single-vintage wines made from one grape varietal. They represent a unique moment, and are a celebration of the subtle differences of the year and the idiosyncratic components of the cultivar. These have yet to find huge commercial appeal as most teas are made to satisfy the Japanese market, which has a taste for consistency. But it is easy to see the appeal from the farmer's point of view. Imagine the dedicated artisan who toils the whole year to coax out the most divine expression of her crop before someone buys it and blends it in with numerous other farmers' teas. The expression of the grower's art can get lost in blends.

Enter the single-cultivar offering. At Kettl, we carry more than fifteen varieties of single-cultivar sencha. I am fascinated by the seemingly endless range of flavors and aromas that fall under the umbrella of sencha. Tasting a tea and beginning to understand the factors that have impacted its flavor: this is something I, and our customers, have come to appreciate. Blends cannot teach one the differences between teas from towns in the same prefecture, for example. Just a decade ago, it was not possible for the average drinker of tea to discover how the same cultivar can change in the hands of two different tea producers. We are lucky to now have access to single-cultivar teas—and I hope to continue to celebrate their unique flavors and fascinating stories for years to come.

A NOTE ON CULTIVARS

Tea plants can reproduce by way of tea seed. Tea grown from seed is referred to as zairai. These days teas are mostly crossbred, but zairai is still produced in small amounts. Zairai can be likened to heirloom corn—similar in appearance to the modern product but with none of the genetic consistency. In a field of zairai, the plants' color, shape, and height vary from bush to bush. This tea is notable for its raw power, and some believe it captures the classic flavor profile of green tea enjoyed long ago in Japan.

Crossbreeding took hold as tea farming became more sophisticated. Farmers began to identify the bushes they felt made the most delicious tea, taking cuttings and grafting them to other plants. These hybrids were further bred to produce bushes with a consistent genetic profile—these are cultivars. Aside from color and flavor, these plants were selected for their resistance to frost, insects, and blight. Additionally, each cultivar becomes ready to harvest at a different point during the season—some earlier, some a bit later. This helps growers manage the process of harvesting. They can focus their efforts on one area of the farm and then move in succession, harvesting the cultivars in other areas as they are ready.

To the consumer, single-cultivar senchas provide a fascinating opportunity to taste a singular harvest of tea. Additionally, single cultivars offer a taste of the soil, weather, and unique attributes conferred by a farmer's personal style of production. They are a celebration of the farming season; like wine, some will reflect not so great years, some will reflect great years, and some will reflect once-in-a-lifetime years.

SENCHA: ONE TEA, MANY STYLES

Steaming has a profound impact on the profile of the sencha. And regionally, teas undergo different lengths of steaming to suit the tastes of the locals. Steaming can be broken down into three main categories:

Asamushi: Asamushi refers to tea that undergoes the least amount of steaming. Asamushi is easily recognizable by its long, slender, needle-shaped leaves. A steaming time of less than fifteen seconds would be considered asamushi. Teas that are less steamed maintain more cellulose in the leaf, allowing them to stand up to the repeated rolling of the aracha and shiage process. The flavor of asamushi can best be summed up as fresh and invigorating with a lively aroma reminiscent of just-harvested leaves. Asamushi is prized for its pristine dry leaf shape and also its fine, light, and radiant yellow liquor. Most competition-level senchas, known as hinpyoukai, are asamushis. Notable areas of production include Uji in Kyoto Prefecture; the mountainous areas of Shizuoka Prefecture including Kawane, Honyama, and Shimizu; and the Kirishima area in Kagoshima Prefecture.

Chuumushi: Representing most likely the largest swath of senchas, chuumushi, or futsumushi, is medium- or "regular"-steamed sencha. This tea is steamed for about twenty to thirty seconds and produces a deeper-colored tea. Chuumushi can run the gamut from low quality to very-high quality. If you have had sencha, it is quite likely you have drunk this style. Depending on the exact processing methods, the dry leaf of chuumushi sencha tends to be very aromatic. The brewed tea can range from neon green to nearly opaque. Notable areas of production include Yame in Fukuoka Prefecture; Shizuoka Prefecture; Mie Prefecture; Kumamoto Prefecture; and Miyazaki Prefecture.

Fukamushi: Fukamushi translates to "deep steamed," and fukamushi senchas are steamed the longest. Fukamushi has grown in popularity for its soft taste, wildly deep green color, and ease of brewing. The tea leaf is broken into smaller bits with more surface area exposed; therefore more of the vibrant green chlorophyll comes through in the brew. Fukamushi is a great entry point to sencha as it is an easy brewer with a mild, approachable profile. Notable areas of production are Shizuoka Prefecture, primarily Kakegawa and Makinohara; Saitama Prefecture, especially Saitama city; and Chiran in Kagoshima Prefecture.

BREWING SENCHA

Brewing a proper cup of sencha is the first thing any Japanese-tea enthusiast should learn to do. When brewed correctly, it can provide that "ah-ha" experience. Sencha provides all of the touch points of a classic Japanese tea experience—sweet, savory, astringent, aromatic, and visually appealing.

A note on brewing: without making things overly complicated, I must stress that every tea you brew will have its own *sweet spot*. Kettl provides tailored brewing parameters for each tea we sell. So please take the guidelines we present here as—well, guidelines. Our suggestions will provide you with an experience that is what you would get in Japan—more leaf, less water, and a richer profile. While everyone has the freedom to make tea the way they like, I suggest trying our method to understand how sencha is meant to be experienced.

A note on water: Water could be a chapter unto itself. We suggest using soft, natural spring water where available. Otherwise, always use fresh filtered water and bring it to a rolling boil in either a traditional stovetop kettle or an electric kettle. Notice we say boil first. The act of boiling the water fully helps to oxygenate it and will lead to a richer, more flavorful brew.

BUYING SENCHA

Like all Japanese tea, sencha must be fresh. Actually, freshness is the key factor in an enjoyable sencha. Unfortunately, almost all commercially available sencha outside of Japan is not fresh. So, buying from a reputable source is the key to finding fresh, flavorful tea. When shopping for sencha, the more information available about the tea, the better the odds are that you are getting something well made. The prefecture of origin should always be available. Ask the tea seller where the tea you're interested in comes from, who grew it, and what distinguishes it as special. Why did they choose it? The more detailed the information provided to you, the better. Sencha should always be sold in opaque packaging, preferably either vacuum sealed or packed with an oxygen absorber. If your tea seller refrigerates her tea, that is also a great sign. Ask what season the tea was harvested. Remember, the highest-quality sencha is made during the early harvest season, which in Japan is from April to May. So for example, teas produced in May of 2022 will be drank until April 2023. And the fresh shincha will arrive again in May of 2023.

STORING SENCHA

Once you open a package of sencha, keep it stored in a opaque container, such as a chazutsu tea caddy, or tightly sealed in the bag it came in. If you drink tea daily and move through it quickly, keeping your tea in a canister out of the fridge is fine. Refrigerate unopened or resealed bags of tea that you will not consume quickly. Sencha that is opened and exposed to air should be consumed as quickly as possible—within about ten to fourteen days for optimal freshness.

For any tea drinker, sencha offers a compelling world of discovery, with new products introduced to the marketplace each year. Whether it's a blend or a single-cultivar tea, something deep and rich or light and floral, my hope is that you will discover the sencha that suits your taste.

Recipe

SENCHA FOR TWO

DIRECTIONS

1. Boil water and let it cool a bit. If you have a temperature-control tea kettle, set it to hold the water at around 190°F (90°C).
2. Pour 250 mL (8.5 fl. oz.) of hot water into your empty teapot and allow it to sit for one minute.
3. Pour the water from the teapot into two empty tea cups. This will preheat the cups and keep the brewed tea at the proper temperature.
4. Add 5–7 g of leaf to your teapot. I like 7 g for a richer taste.
5. After the water has cooled in the cups to around 175°F (75°C), pour it into the teapot that contains the leaves.
6. Brew for 1 minute.
7. Pour the tea, making sure to alternate between the cups as you pour.

CHAPTER FIVE

Matcha

THE POPULARITY OF MATCHA WAS ON THE RISE DURING THE last decade, and today matcha is the most consumed Japanese green tea outside of Japan. In fact, sales of matcha in the US have increased a staggering fivefold in twenty-five years. While it's easy to find information about matcha on the internet, I've learned from conversations with matcha professionals in Japan that much of that information is incomplete, misleading, or false.

So, what exactly is matcha? Simply put, matcha (抹茶) is a green tea that has undergone intentional shading and is stone milled into a fine powder. Matcha is prepared by whisking the powder with hot water in a tea bowl to create a fine foam. Although its origins lie in China, today matcha production is unique to Japan. Matcha maintains its storied place in the canon of Japanese teas for many reasons, but the most obvious is that it is the tea used in the Japanese tea ceremony. Furthermore, its preparation is singular: matcha powder is whisked into a suspended state with a fine foam on top and then drank directly from a tea bowl. Therefore, the entire leaf is consumed. Currently, high-grade matcha is produced exclusively in Japan with the highest grades coming from Uji just south of Kyoto, Yame in Fukuoka Prefecture, and *(continued on p. 86)*

Interview

KIYOHARU
TSUJI

Kiyoharu Tsuji's name is synonymous with Uji matcha. His commitment to both tradition and innovation in forty years of matcha production has led to his earning more awards in the field of tea than anyone else in Japan. His accolades include six awards from Japan's Ministry of Agriculture and Forest and Fisheries as well as the 56th Prime Minister's Award for Excellence in Agriculture. Tsuji-san resides near his farm in Shirakawa, Uji.

Zach Mangan: You are so highly awarded and have accomplished so much in your career. What do you see for the future of matcha production?

Kiyoharu Tsuji: This is true. But I am confident in the future. I am fifth-generation, and my son, who is twenty-four, will be the sixth generation. He was working in a bank but saw that our family's tea was loved by customers, and their compliments fueled our passion and productivity. And he became interested in that cycle and decided, on his own, to leave the bank and come produce tea.

And I am sure that made you happy?

I was. Actually, I established what we have now, but I am very happy to know that the person who protects our tea farm after me is my son. Since I never give him a lecture, he finds things by himself, talks to the plants, observes them every day, adds fertilizers, has conversations with the plants to find out how they are doing and what kind of tea he is going to get. I've had such conversations with the plants many times and won many awards. Anyone can do what they are told, but it's important to notice something on your own without being told, so I told my son to learn from tea.

How do you balance tradition with a drive for continual growth and development?

Growing conditions for tea differ every year. This gives me a chance to assess what incremental changes I can make—and then I can map their effect in the outcome of the year's tea. This has been my method for thirty years. I keep the main pillar of tradition and always experiment with 10 to 30 percent of the variables. This way I can preserve tradition and still make breakthroughs

That is an inspiring viewpoint.

Yes. Uji tea's pillar was built on tradition. French wine won't fail because the industry has both respect for the tradition and willingness to take on challenges. So, in many ways we model ourselves on that idea.

What is your desert-island tea?

Of course, absolutely matcha!

YOSHITSUGU AND MIZUHO FURUKAWA

Yoshitsugu and Mizuho Furukawa, a husband-and-wife team, craft small-batch, single-cultivar matcha next to the banks of the Uji river in Gokasho. Both humble and charming, they'd never let on that they have been awarded Japan's top prize for matcha. But everyone who knows them says the same thing: They never cut corners, and you can taste their passion in the tea they make. In addition to producing peerless matcha, they have a deep respect for their land and act as its stewards. They have begun practicing an all-natural form of garden management and document their processes on social media. Year after year they quietly craft teas of the highest order, helping all discover the magic of nature.

Zach Mangan: How long has your family been producing tea in Uji?

Yoshitsugu Furukawa: I am fifth or sixth generation. But since our farm is on the banks of the Uji river, all documents about the family were washed away in a flood. But all farmers here are about fifth or sixth generation as prior to that, it was outlawed to grow tea by the shogunate in Edo. As the shogunate's power weakened, farmers began to produce tea. That is the history of Uji and our own personal history as well.

And the history of honzu (straw reed) shading is based here as well, no?

There is no real written history of the exact origins. But a Portuguese missionary spoke of tea being covered with straw and reeds in his book *Nihonkyoukaishi* (*The history of the church in Japan*) in the year 1580.

Do you still believe honzu is superior?

Well, it is hard to say. Kanreisha (made from chemical fibers) has improved, but so has the breeding of cultivars and the fertilizers. So, it is very difficult to isolate one element from another. But I value tradition and continue to use honzu on portions of my farm.

How else do you feel the flavor of matcha has changed over the years?

Tea processing was much slower historically—so tea leaves usually sat for a while before being steamed. The leaves actually underwent a bit of withering, of oxidation. So matcha made one or two hundred years ago would have had a strong floral aroma. And of course, more astringency. I have been fascinated by this and have even started to make "ichou" matcha, which is allowed to wither a bit. I think it is interesting to try to create tea of the past.

What is your desert-island tea?

Oh, I would want to drink lots and lots of tea—so I would take houjicha or bancha.

The many textures of matcha

Nishio in Aichi Prefecture. The lesser-known areas that produce matcha are Shizuoka and Kagoshima Prefectures.

I first experienced matcha while working for a Japanese tea company out of college. When I started I was well versed in steeping tea, but I was unfamiliar with matcha and so I was unsure how to make it (a sentiment I hear often). So, a coworker offered to show me. As she brought out the tools for making matcha, I was immediately drawn to the beauty of the chasen bamboo whisk, and the balance of the chawan tea bowl in my hands. The choreographed steps of preparing the tea were like taking a deep breath—it was exhilarating to put away my thoughts for a minute and focus on something so serene. Pour hot water into the bowl, pour out. Pat dry the bowl with a cloth. Sift in the matcha powder. Slowly add water. Whisk vigorously. Carefully raise the bowl to your lips. Simplicity. But the flavor: it was a rush of intense freshness that filled my whole nose and mouth. And the texture: creamy while being both sweet and savory. There was also something so fleeting about it. Three sips and it's over. So, I made an awkward attempt to make my own bowl. And another. I drank five bowls of matcha that day. It was also a great lesson in the caffeine content of matcha (see chapter 14)—I don't think I slept that night, or maybe the next night either. But that was fine, just more time to think about how fascinating this drink was that was so new to me.

Matcha has a long history in Japan that is intricately intertwined with the Japanese tea ceremony, part of an aesthetic pursuit referred to as chado, "the way of tea." Chado's cultural roots can be traced back to the fifteenth century with the development of shoin chanoyu by Ashikaga Yoshimasa. Shoin referred to a den or alcove used by Buddhist priests and monks to gather and spend leisure time together. This room was the first to contain many of the most famous elements associated with a Japanese tearoom: tatami bamboo flooring, washi-papered sliding doors, and an alcove for a small scroll or flower arrangement. This was the first step toward the formal tearooms developed later by Takeno Jōō and most famously Sen no Rikyū. And it was here that matcha grew from a powdered medicine into a refined drink that in many ways represents the heart and soul of Japan.

The tools of matcha—chasen, chawan, and chashaku

TENCHA: THE BUILDING BLOCK OF MATCHA

Before matcha is whisked in your bowl, it has to be carefully grown and processed. In actuality, farmers don't grow matcha, they grow tencha, the raw leaf material that is milled to create matcha. So matcha is really ground tencha. Tencha farming is a very labor-intensive profession. But in certain areas—especially Uji in the Kyoto region—gyokuro farmers are transitioning to growing tencha as the global demand for matcha outpaces that of gyokuro many times over. Tencha production is quite specialized work and requires fierce commitment. I have found that tencha farming is more like a calling than a job. The dedication from the growers I have met is palpable. Knowing that the highest grades of tencha will be milled and used in Japanese tea ceremonies likely adds a certain gravity to the work of producing each year's harvest.

Similarly to gyokuro, tencha is made by shading unpruned tea bushes under tana coverings for between twenty-five to forty days. The style of using unpruned versus pruned tea plants is referred to as shizenshitate—and the plants are either shaded by kanreisha, a type of synthetic netting, or honzu, natural rice straw scattered over bamboo trellises. The shading process creates a low-light environment that impacts the tea plants in four main ways and has a tremendous effect on the outcome of the tea. First, the shaded plant produces more chlorophyll to capture the little light that is available to it. This accounts for matcha's deep verdant

MATCHA

FLAVOR PROFILE:
The flavor is savory and grassy with aromas ranging
from nutty and creamy to marine-like

ESTABLISHED PRODUCTION AREAS INCLUDE:
Kyoto Prefecture: Uji
Fukuoka Prefecture
Kagoshima Prefecture: Chiran, Kirishima

EMERGING PRODUCTION AREAS INCLUDE:
Shizuoka Prefecture: Okabe
Kagoshima Prefecture: Kirishima

Spreading straw during honzu shading, Ogura City, Uji, Kyoto

color and unique aroma. Second, as the plant searches for light it grows upward, and each leaf extends outward exposing its entire surface area. The leaf becomes soft and pliable. This accounts for matcha's incredible silky texture. The third effect directly impacts matcha's flavor. During normal photosynthesis a tea plant converts its amino acids into catechin, a type of antioxidant. But a plant receiving less sunlight begins to change on a cellular level. Its conversion of amino acids, like theanine, into catechin slows. Theanine, glutamate, and arginine build up in the leaves of the plant. This spectrum of chemicals accounts for the intense umami of high-quality matcha. Lastly, as energy from the sun above becomes less available, the tea plant begins to rely more on energy from the soil, bringing as much energy as it can up through its root system. Producers must ensure their soil can provide the nutrients their plants need to grow. Specific nitrogen-rich fertilizers derived from fish meal and soybean cake are ideal. The tencha cultivar, the method and length of its shading, and the composition of the soil and fertilizer used in its cultivation all combine to create the terroir of each matcha. These are the main factors that impact the flavor of the tea prior to manufacturing.

Depending on the region, the tencha harvest begins in early to mid-May when the young tea leaves have sprouted and the shading process is complete.

The highest-quality tenchas are picked by hand. This ensures that only the leaf and buds will be selected and very little stem detritus will make its way into the tea pickers' baskets. For teas produced in larger volumes, machine harvesting is more popular. Machine harvesting is faster and less expensive. A harvest can be completed in a quarter of the time it would take by hand with only two people. Handpicking, by contrast, requires a team of experienced tea pickers. Once the leaf is picked, the harvest is swiftly transported to a tencha factory to undergo a unique set of processing steps.

Processing takes place in a tencha kojo, or tencha factory. Large tea companies and wholesalers generally own their own factories and use them exclusively to produce their own teas. Smaller companies and independent farmers generally rely on shared factories in a sort of time-share arrangement. Some farmers will run the factory and all the machines in it by themselves—which is an incredible feat. Often, farmers will help each other. When one grower's tea is being harvested, other farmers will assist, and the next day it will be another farmer's day to get assistance. But regardless of whether the factory is privately owned or shared, the process of making tencha remains pretty constant.

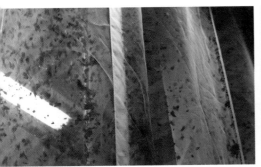

Left: Kakusan reikyaku, the process of cooling the steamed tencha leaf
Right: Ara kanso, a critical step in drying tencha

As with all Japanese green tea, tencha processing begins when the freshly picked leaves are steamed to deactivate any oxidative enzymes. Producers must keep a watchful eye, as this step is one that will determine a tea's final color—a matter of huge importance. The steaming process is something that only happens once a year, and visiting the factory during this time electrifies the senses. The entire factory is filled with the heady aroma of steamed leaves—a fresh and intoxicating smell reminiscent of lemon balm, ripe fruit, and sweet grass. Each step must be completed on time and the movement to the next step is of great importance. After steaming comes kakusan reikyaku, a cooling of the tea leaves. This is perhaps the most unique looking of almost any tea-making process in Japan. The leaves are blown up a succession of twenty-foot columns made from netting. In addition to cooling the leaves this process allows any residual moisture on their surface to dissipate. The machines that do this job are uncommon and only used in tencha factories. But this step must be completed if the tea being produced can claim to be "true" matcha. The next step is equally unique. Tencha factories have large, brick ovens that resemble long pizza ovens. The leaves move through them slowly on a conveyor belt, and as they do they are dried both by the heat and by infrared radiation produced by the heated bricks. The first phase of drying, called ara kanso, takes place at about 150°C, while the second phase, hon kanso, takes place at a cooler temperature, around 100°C. This baking process is critical and removes even more moisture from the leaf. Additionally, the aromatic compounds in the tea intensify in the heat, imbuing the leaves with a rich fragrance. Each producer has a specific duration for heating and drying that she believes is best and rarely shares the exact parameters with others, much like how a baker might guard the secrets to his exact baking times. At this point, the teas are beginning to resemble the final tencha, but they still contain stems, coarse leaves, and other detritus. A sorting step removes the unwanted stems and other matter, leaving behind only the choicest leaves. It is critical that the tencha leaves are all a uniform shape and size as any variance will make the final stone milling difficult. After sorting, a final drying process, called neri kanso, lowers the moisture level further, to roughly

3 to 5 percent. At this point the tencha is stable enough to be aged, or if desired, milled. Some competition-level tencha destined for the National Tea Fair will go on to a final sorting where leaves are separated further by size. This is done by a team using tweezers and discerning eyes. Labor-intensive is an understatement—hand sorting is grueling. But uniform flecks of deep green tencha, once processed, are breathtaking.

The final step before milling is perhaps the most mysterious and a little hard to explain. It is called jukusei, which refers to the process of resting or aging the tencha. The term jukusei is also used by Japanese chefs to describe the process of aging fish or meat, and in reality the goals with tencha are the same. Un-aged tencha is full of amino acids, and a resting period in cold storage mellows the flavor and tends to add a layer of depth. It should be noted that jukusei is employed more in the Kyoto area than in Kyushu. The distinct aroma that develops with a bit of age is adored by tea wholesalers and customers alike in Kyoto; an ambrosial, almost fruity floral note replaces the piercing grassiness you get if you mill tencha right after spring processing. Jukusei also intensifies umami and accentuates some of the more "marine" aromas present in the tea. Think toasted nori seaweed, oysters, and salty ocean air.

Producers in Fukuoka have a different point of view on jukusei. In general, they control the fragrance of their tea by applying heat before milling. This slightly caramelizes the sugars present in the tea plant and adds a layer of depth while maintaining a fresh spring-grass aroma.

Left: Tencha being stone milled *Center:* Matcha immediately after milling
Right: A fresh tin of matcha

What's achieved is a more chocolaty, nutty, and umami-rich profile without aging. This limits to a degree the development of more oceanic aromas. All of this combined represents the preferred flavor profile of Kyushu-style matcha.

The next step is shared in all regions that produce high-quality matcha: stone milling. This step is of supreme importance, as matcha's defining characteristic is that it is milled. Tencha is usually blended before milling in a ratio that is consistent and repeatable, ensuring customers get the flavor they expect month after month, year after year. Once the tencha is blended it is loaded into a metal funnel that sits over two circular slabs of granite. These granite slabs each have a specific pattern etched into them. When the mill is turned on, the top slab slowly rotates clockwise while the bottom slab remains fixed in place. Most high-quality producers of matcha will use a specific type of granite sourced from Aichi Prefecture. The material is important: granite stays cool despite the friction from grinding. This is key as even low levels of heat can alter the subtle fragrance and color of matcha powder. One mill produces between thirty to forty grams of matcha powder per hour. For this reason, larger-scale producers will usually have dozens of mills operating around the clock. Of course, a smaller-scale farmer may utilize one or two mills and mill when needed or rent space at a larger factory for big orders. Milled matcha powder is incredibly sensitive to light, heat, air, and moisture—so most milling rooms are air conditioned and operate with the lights off to protect the delicate tea. The milled matcha is deposited in a steel box below the granite and is collected throughout the day. It is critical that the matcha is packed in an oxygen-free bag or tin shortly after milling to maintain freshness. Once the matcha is packed in its retail packaging it is refrigerated before shipment.

MATCHA PRODUCTION REGIONS
Uji, Kyoto
There is simply no other place on earth more important to matcha than Uji. It is the cultural, commercial, and spiritual home of matcha. To this day, Uji is known in all corners of Japan as a producer of peerless

matcha—as well as other green teas. The history of Uji tea is long and complicated, but in essence, the techniques for growing and producing matcha were established here. And the Japanese tea ceremony was codified in neighboring Kyoto. So, the intersection of tea and Japanese culture is a way of life in Uji.

Uji is nestled in a valley between the Tamba Highlands and the Yamashiro basin and is positioned on the banks of the Uji river. The river provides consistent temperature and humidity levels throughout the year—favorable for growing quality green tea. The silty, sandy soil on the banks of the river is where much of the tencha in Uji is grown. City quarters like Gokasho and Ogura are known to produce teas with incredible color and clarity. Seeing these areas dappled with small swatches of green tea fields is a reminder that Uji was built to accommodate tea production. Other notable areas of tencha production in Uji are Shirakawa, Kyōtanabe, and Ujitawara. Many of the families producing tea in these areas have been doing so for centuries, and their depth and breadth of knowledge exists nowhere outside of Uji. Even the tea sellers in town have a deep history: Tsuen, a tea shop next to the Uji Bridge, is the oldest continually operating tea shop in Japan and has been there since 1160, ranking among the thirty oldest continually operating businesses in the world. This incredible history is palpable, and sellers at Tsuen demonstrate a depth of knowledge and understanding of matcha production that cannot be found anywhere else.

In addition to being home to matcha's art and craft, Uji is also its commercial heart. The tea industry in Uji is vibrant, with many farmers, wholesalers, and tea shops working together with a single vision to promote Uji tea. While Uji is a small place, some of the most esteemed tea growers and producers are based there. To understand the quality level of tea here, we can take a look at the 2020 All Japan Top Tea list. In the category of tencha, Uji teas took spots one through forty-six. Fukuoka came in at forty-seven. In addition to farms, many factories dealing in direct trade are based in and around Uji. These factories are home to chashi—tea professionals responsible for not only growing tea but also buying and blending other farmers' teas. Some of Japan's oldest and most esteemed tea families still operate in Uji today.

Yame, Fukuoka

Fukuoka Prefecture is a relative newcomer to matcha production but hasn't wasted any time developing into a small but mighty production region. The bulk of high-quality tencha from Fukuoka is produced in the deep mountainous areas of Yame—mainly Hoshinomura, Kurogi, and Yabemura. Although the production output is much smaller than that of Uji, Yame's success as a producer of the finest gyokuro in Japan has helped inform its approach to creating pinnacle-grade matcha. With such a short history of producing matcha, Yame producers do not benefit from the history, depth of knowledge, or industrial infrastructure enjoyed by producers in Uji. But this is also a silver lining: it has allowed Yame to innovate and create its own path forward. I remember sitting with an esteemed tea producer in Uji. We were looking at a magazine that featured a matcha from Yame produced using a certain cultivar, Okumidori, that would never be used in Uji. The producer looked at the magazine in disbelief. "That is simply not real matcha if they are using Okumidori," he said. The very same day I visited a young farmer in Uji to taste some of his tea. And when he discovered that Kettl also sold Yame

matcha, he quickly stepped into the back of his shop and returned with the very same can of matcha that was in the magazine. He looked at me and said, "I can't say this out loud to anyone in Uji, but this matcha is so interesting—and delicious! We could never make this here in Uji, but I have been drinking it daily, and to be honest, I love it." This to me characterizes the charm of a "newer" region of production like Yame. It can develop outside of the rigid structures of established production regions and incorporate know-how of other styles of tea to make delicious matcha. When it began, the quality of Yame matcha was low and the farmers were laughed at for trying. But year after year, with hard work and determination, its quality grew. And today, the popularity of Fukuoka matcha has grown tremendously within Japan. Even the tea schools in Kyoto and Tokyo are using Yame matcha in tea ceremonies—a sure testament to the quality of the tea and the tireless work of the Fukuoka tea industry.

Nishio, Aichi

Nishio in Aichi Prefecture is an esteemed region of matcha. In fact, more than 90 percent of the green tea produced in Nishio is tencha—the building block of matcha. Nishio lies on the shores of Mikawa (continued on p. 101)

MOTOHARU
KOYAMA

Motoharu Koyama is the president and lead chashi, or tea blender, of the famed Uji company Marukyu Koyamaen. His family's history in tea and his fierce commitment to quality set him in a class of his own. His company is responsible for buying and blending more tea in the Uji area than anyone else. Koyama-san's keen sense means he buys only the best leaves, and any farmer lucky enough to work with him mentions his name with the deepest respect. He grants very few interviews, so I was thrilled to spend time with Koyama-san and learn more about the deep history of his company and what is so special about being a chashi.

Zach Mangan: Can you tell us a bit about the history of your company?

Motoharu Koyama: We first started our tea plantation here in Ogura [Uji] in the Genroku period (1688–1704). And then we began selling tea at the end of the Edo period and have been in business since. From the start, our company has focused on "quality-first" tea making. We have been committed to that idea from generation to generation, with a motto to make tea that makes our customers happy and has unsurpassed quality.

Do you still farm your own teas as well?

Yes, in addition to working with farmers we own our own farm. And though I can't really plow the field myself anymore, I sometimes still help pulling weeds. Having our own fields allows me to see the condition of the year's harvest—the impact of weather and such—and understand more what the other farmers we work with are experiencing. I get to know the quality of the season's products and understand the struggles of the farmers. Also, when I price the tea brought in by the contracted farmers, the knowledge I've learned by owning my own farm and observing the conditions can be helpful. This makes me more confident about setting prices and

that leads to the farmers' trust. And I think that's why everyone feels safe working with Koyamaen.

Can you tell me a bit about the tea-blending process?

The process is different depending on, for example, the soil the tea was grown in. Even here in Kyoto, the tea grown in sandy soil by the river has better color, but the taste is lighter. Tea grown in mixed red soil near the mountain doesn't have good color but smells good. And the taste gets thicker and better in fall. And the taste of tea grown in sand is light while the taste of tea grown in red soil is thick. If we blend those teas we get something in the middle. We must focus on color, aroma, and flavor—so with all the different characteristics of the teas we grow and bid on, it certainly gets complicated. We don't just blend once a year—we blend monthly. Having a higher volume of various teas makes it easier to blend consistently as we have more variation to rely on. In order to be successful you need to buy a lot so you are not beholden to just one or two flavor profiles. And as a company, this is our strong point: We know what teas to buy and truly understand how to combine them.

Do you work alone, or with other members of your company?

The team is my son and five others. We are in charge of different divisions, but each tea, everyone drinks. At least three people drink it. I can't do it by myself, and if only two people drink it, it can be biased. It works with three people… if I'm not feeling well, I might not distinguish correctly when we are sampling one hundred kinds of tea.

And the final judge is…

The final judgment about a tea would be made by me though. Most of the time when we price a tea, five of us do it. And more often than not, the average price of all of us matches my price. Probably 90 percent of the time.

Left: The patterns in the stone mill are critical to the fine grind produced.
Right: Matcha being stone milled, Fukuoka Prefecture

Bay. Nestled along the Yahagi River, the flatlands of Nishio benefit from cooler air temperatures and well-draining silt soil. While Nishio doesn't benefit from the presence of rolling hills or mountains, the fog created by the Yahagi River allows for rolling mist to cover the fields, and naturally diffuse sunlight provides a cooler environment in which the tea leaves can grow slowly and condense flavor and nutrients. While Nishio produces some very high-quality matcha, in recent years it has increased its output significantly to cater to the demand for culinary-grade matcha used in sweets, ice creams, flavorings, and supplements. In early 2020 it went so far as to renounce its Geographical Indication (GI) protection, effectively allowing increased flexibility in what constitutes "Nishio matcha." This has allowed more shading and milling techniques to be employed, lowering the cost of the tea so as to make it more attractive on an international scale.

SINGLE CULTIVARS

In recent years, as with sencha, single-cultivar matcha has become more widely available. In the past, a farmer's job was to grow tencha and sell it to a chashi who would blend the tea to make a house matcha that was consistent year over year. Basically, the farmer produced the raw materials for the chashi. The growing popularity of single-cultivar matcha has allowed farmers to showcase their skill and mastery in an undiluted format. The joy of being able to try a farmer's tea unblended is that it allows you to taste the flavor of the cultivar, the charm of the soil, and the impact that the farmer's choices during harvest and manufacture have on the final product. You can really enjoy the terroir of matcha in a whole new way.

The cultivars used to grow tencha vary by region, but here is a list of some of the most well known.

Asahi—A native Uji cultivar and without a doubt, the pinot noir of tencha. Asahi commands the highest price at auction, and when grown well it showcases the power, finesse, and fragrance of pinnacle-grade matcha. With a shallower root system than many other cultivars, Asahi can be fickle and hard to please. But under the watchful eye of a seasoned producer, it can create a magical matcha.

Uji Hikari—Another native Uji cultivar. Uji Hikari is often used for gyokuro production but in recent years has become more popular for matcha. Uji Hikari has a powerful aroma and can develop a deep, long-lasting umami that is sought after in high-end matcha.

Samidori—The most widely produced cultivar in Uji. It skews toward the "less challenging" column when it comes to growing. It produces matcha with a lighter body and a consistent green color. This is often the building block for blended matcha and, unless grown by a farmer with great care, can sometimes feel a bit boring on its own.

Saemidori—A rich and vibrant cultivar that produces a pleasing sweetness and a gyokuro-like umami. A great place to start for approachable, rewarding matcha.

Gokou—A cultivar that, like Uji Hikari, has been used primarily for gyokuro. It has a unique aroma that is almost floral with a punchy, grassy finish.

BLENDING FOR CONSISTENCY: THE JOB OF THE CHASHI

While single-cultivar matcha has increased in popularity the last few years, in most cases, matcha is actually a blend. Much like the cuvée wines of Bordeaux in which multiple types of grapes are blended to create a beloved profile, matcha too is made from a blend of tenchas. This process is driven by customers' expectations that they will receive the same product year-over-year. And the most discerning customers in Japan are the traditional tea ceremony schools. They go so far as to select special blends that become famous at each school. Consistency is paramount—upsetting the customers is not an option. So, on whom does this responsibility fall? The chashi. Chashi are tea blenders whose job it is to select, buy, and blend tencha to create teas with profiles that do

Left: Asahi cultivar, Uji, Kyoto
Right: Uji Hikari cultivar, Uji, Kyoto. The leaves create a star shape due to shading.

not change between batches. A chashi's company may grow some of its own tencha, but much of it is typically bought at auction. The auction system in Japan allows farmers to bring their products to a central place so tea producers can bid on it. Each year in the spring, teas are evaluated by the chashi using sight, smell, taste, and touch. What might seem like imperceptible details of the teas are easily detected by the trained senses of a master blender. In almost all cases, the chashi works with a team to evaluate, blend, and create each product. From there, teas are blended and tasted constantly, and small changes and tweaks are made throughout the year. It really cannot be overstated how much skill and patience this job entails. It is a practice I have been in awe of since I first traveled to Japan, and I remain in awe of it today.

TOOLS FOR A PERFECT MATCHA

1. *Chawan:* A chawan, or tea bowl, is an essential item. A chawan serves as the vessel for both preparing and drinking your matcha. Chawan are at the heart of the tea ceremony and for good reason—they're beautiful and richly rewarding to use. Find a bowl that speaks to you and use it regularly.

2. *Chasen:* This hand-carved bamboo whisk is a must for achieving level-ten foam. Wire whisks, forks, spoons—trust me—they don't work. Get one!

3. *Chasen naoshi:* The chasen naoshi is a stand for drying your whisk and allowing it to keep its shape. A chasen naoshi will double the life of your chasen.

4. *Chashaku:* A bamboo scoop perfectly calibrated at .5 g per scoop. Three-to-four scoops and you've got the perfect amount of matcha.

5. *Furui:* Matcha is so finely ground that it tends to clump due to static charge. Running the matcha through a furui sifter will ensure a perfectly smooth, clump-free matcha.

BUYING MATCHA

Your matcha should list Japan as the country of origin. Ideally, it should list a region, town, and grower, but most basically, your matcha should come from Japan. In no uncertain terms, true matcha is a Japanese product. Other countries that produce "matcha" are providing you with powdered green tea of uncertain quality. Japan follows accepted *(continued on p. 108)*

Recipe

USUCHA: THIN MATCHA

Usucha is the most well-known preparation of matcha. It is whisked to create a fine microfoam providing a rich and refreshing experience.

DIRECTIONS

1. Bring your water to a full boil and then pour 65 mL (2.25 fl. oz.) into a small cup to cool slightly.
2. Pour hot water into an empty chawan. Wait several seconds before emptying the warmed chawan and patting dry with a clean towel.
3. Scoop 1.5–2 g of matcha into a furui over your empty chawan and sift.
4. Once the water in your cup has cooled to around 170–180°F (77–82°C), add it to the matcha powder.
5. Gently knead the matcha into the water and then whisk in a vigorous Z pattern until a foam appears.
6. Lift your chasen to the surface of the foam and continue gently whisking to create a microfoam. Support your bowl from the bottom, raise to your lips, and enjoy.

Recipe

THICK MATCHA

Koicha is much less known outside of the traditional Japanese tea ceremony. It is a luxurious style of matcha made with a higher ratio of powder to water.

DIRECTIONS

1. Bring your water to a full boil and then pour 30–35 mL (1–1.15 fl. oz.) into a small cup to cool slightly.
2. Pour hot water into an empty chawan. Wait several seconds before emptying the warmed chawan and patting dry with a clean towel.
3. Scoop 4 g of matcha into a furui over your empty chawan and sift.
4. Once the water in your cup cools to around 180°F (82°C), add half to the matcha powder.
5. Use the chasen to gently knead the matcha into the water without vigorous whisking. The aim is to make a smooth paste free of any clumps.
6. Add the remaining water and continue to knead until the tea is the texture of paint.
7. Enjoy the thick tea. When you are finished you can add 30 mL (1 fl. oz.) of hot water and whisk the matcha that has settled into a frothy bowl of usucha.

Recipe

KETTL MATCHA LATTE

DIRECTIONS

1. Combine 4 g of sifted matcha with 50 mL
   (1.75 fl. oz.) of hot water.
2. Vigorously whisk the matcha in a Z pattern
   until a fine foam appears (approx. 15–20 seconds).
3. Steam 220 mL (7.5 fl. oz.) of milk (or milk
   alternative).
4. Combine, stir, and serve.
5. Enjoy!

guidelines for its growing, manufacturing, and milling—and the combination of old-world expertise and modern technology makes Japan the only country of origin for acceptable matcha. Origins inside Japan can be Uji Prefecture, Fukuoka Prefecture (Yame), Aichi Prefecture (Nishio), and more recently Kagoshima and Shizuoka Prefectures (often for organic).

Good matcha has a best-by date. Drinking expensive, refined matcha means nothing if the product is not fresh. Matcha is not like wine and does not benefit from age or vintage. Once the leaf is ground, it should be consumed as quickly as possible. Reputable sellers will list the best-by date—generally on the bottom of the can or printed on the bag. If it is not there, there is no way to know when the matcha was produced or when it should be consumed by.

The best matcha will be packed in a small tin or foil bag (often in a tin) and include an oxygen absorber inside. Again, these may seem like small things, but matcha is very finely ground, meaning more of the product's total surface area is exposed to air at all times, and its flavor can degrade in a matter of days.

Matcha should be refrigerated prior to sale. When buying over the internet it can be hard to know how a company stores its matcha, but you can always ask. If you see matcha being refrigerated at a tea shop, that is a sign that the retailer understands the importance of taking care of their product. Case in point, even the smallest local tea shops in Japan refrigerate their tea.

STORING MATCHA

Well-made matcha is not cheap, so it is important to protect your investment by keeping it fresh. After buying matcha, keep the unopened package in the refrigerator. At the shop we often get asked if the freezer is better, but freezing your matcha is not necessary. After opening your matcha always securely screw the lid back on the tin or reseal the bag. You can then store the tin or bag inside a Ziploc bag and keep that in the refrigerator. Be careful when taking the matcha powder in and out of the fridge. If your kitchen is particularly hot or humid you can risk condensation buildup on the lid, which can lead to the degradation of your matcha. But this does not happen often under normal weather conditions.

A FINAL WORD ON MATCHA

It is easy to see the appeal of matcha—while both delicious and healthy, it also provides a glimpse of traditional Japan. With its rich history and vibrant industry, matcha will continue to grow in popularity as more and more customers find and embrace it. And as the industry continues to develop to keep up with demand, the responsibility for its next phase lies with the tea sellers abroad. The days of putting any old matcha on a website and claiming fantastical health benefits are over. Customers now demand more detailed information and their palates demand a certain level of quality. So education and proper sourcing will become more and more important to any business hoping to keep its more sophisticated customers happy. And for those of us who have been impassioned about sharing great teas and the stories that surround them, this is music to our ears.

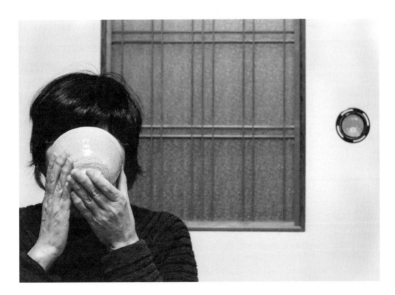

CHAPTER SIX

Gyokuro

GYOKURO IS A SPECIAL TEA WHOSE IDENTITY IS WHOLLY AND completely Japanese; but if you ask most citizens of Japan if they are familiar with gyokuro or whether they have had it properly prepared for them, the answer will likely be "no." When you realize gyokuro accounts for less than .05 percent of Japan's yearly total tea production, it's not so hard to imagine why most Japanese people are unfamiliar with it, not to mention those of us in the West.

THE SILVER BULLET OF FLAVOR

Gyokuro is a tea that initially eluded me. When I first encountered it at tea shops in the United States, I couldn't understand what differentiated it from sencha. For one, it looked similar. And in most cases the brewing instructions on the back of the packaging were also exactly the same—which is an error on the tea seller's part. These factors, coupled with the fact that the first gyokuro I encountered was not of great quality to begin with, and probably not stored particularly well, made my first few experiences with gyokuro confusing. Why was I paying twice as much as I would for sencha for a similar experience?

It wasn't until I tried gyokuro at Kai, a Japanese restaurant in New York City, in 2008, that I had a "come to Jesus"—or "come to gyokuro"—experience. Gyokuro is brewed in a very peculiar way: with lots of leaf and a very small amount of cool water. When I saw the thimble-size cup of gyokuro being presented to me I thought, "It's more expensive and this is all you get?" But then I had my first sip—and I came to Jesus!

Explaining the experience of your first sip of quality gyokuro is hard. Every week I watch customers take a sip and proclaim, "Whoa! What? Oh my God!" I have a folder in my phone with videos of first-timers drinking gyokuro. Their expressions are amazing—pure wonder and delight. Why? Well, because looking at the small, clear cup of liquid and then tasting the deep, rich, distilled umami, which can only be compared to dashi stock or consommé, scrambles the senses. How can it taste like that? The sweetness, the briny umami, and the delicate aroma of quality gyokuro strikes every flavor note that you would experience during a three-hour meal at Le Bernadin or Sushi Nakazawa, and it happens all at once. Chefs are especially taken by the sophistication of gyokuro's flavor.

Professional chefs have access to the finest ingredients and possess the most refined palates imaginable. Many have traveled extensively and have cataloged experiences of dishes, drinks, and spices from the world over. The startling power and refinement of a single cup of gyokuro seems to move them because it challenges their past experiences of flavor. How could something so simple taste like this? That sense of discovery is what chefs crave, and it has been my pleasure over the last decade to share with them the wonderful surprise that is gyokuro.

Gyokuro exists in a realm that may be more art than beverage. It is not made to quench thirst or warm one up from the cold outside. It is a precious style of tea that is a sincere reflection of cultural respect for the shokunin, or master craftsperson, a touchstone of Japanese culture. It is simultaneously an exercise in nurturing the plant and allowing it to express itself naturally while also gently influencing the plant's environment to produce a unique flavor and aroma. Even its name is a testament to the profound labor involved in crafting it: Gyokuro translates to "precious dew" or "precious drop." Truthfully, gyokuro *(continued on p. 118)*

SHINKI
YAMASHITA

The name Yamashita is synonymous with gyokuro. Shinki Yamashita is young but has already done the family name proud as he tends the same plants he inherited from his grandfather, the legendary Toshikazu Yamashita, whose influence on the gyokuro industry is hard to overstate. He has won more national prizes than any other producer, was awarded the Order of the Sacred Treasure by the office of the prime minister, and was designated a master craftsman of Japan by the Ministry of Labor. Yamashita-san has been guided by his grandfather and is now producing top-tier, prize-winning gyokuro of his own.

Zach Mangan: Can you tell me your family's history?

Shinki Yamashita: My family's history is about one hundred years old. I'm the third generation to own these fields my grandfather Toshikazu-san established. And before him, my great-grandfather Shinichi-san established our family business as the first one to start making gyokuro in Fugenji in Kyōtanabe. We do not make sencha or tencha at all, only gyokuro. It was Shinichi-san's—how should I say—pride, or policy, to master only the taste of gyokuro.

Can you talk a little about Kyōtanabe, where your farm is located?

In Kyōtanabe we basically only make gyokuro. There is a small amount of tencha (matcha) production, but basically it's known for gyokuro. So it's a bit different from the other areas that produce many types of tea. And maybe most importantly the gyokuro is all hand-picked. This is rare: a town where many farmers still continue to make the hand-picked gyokuro.

In your opinion, how does Uji gyokuro production differ from Yame?

I believe how we think about the tea over multiple steepings is different. We value a different approach in Uji than in Yame. Here, we believe the fifth steeping should be as rich in flavor as the first steeping. In Yame,

the first steeping is the most rich, the second is lighter and is meant to cleanse the palate, and the third steep is meant to be the most refreshing. Here, we believe the richness of umami should be consistent and strong from the first to the fifth steep—at least! But the difference in the taste of teas is okay—each can express something different and that is a great thing. Because we appreciate what they do, we can talk like that. And, I think because they appreciate what we do, we can have a great relationship with them.

What is your plan for the future?

To continue making only gyokuro. Right now matcha is rather popular and booming. Even so, what I want to do is make the best gyokuro in Japan until I die. So, I am taking the taste of gyokuro seriously.

What is your desert-island tea?

Kyōtanabe gyokuro, of course!

The author with Toshikazu Yamashita, Yamashita-san's grandfather and perhaps the most influential gyokuro farmer in the modern era.

Interview

MASAHIRO
KUMA

Masahiro Kuma, a shy and soft-spoken gyokuro producer from Yame, became well known in 2017 when he was recognized by the Japanese government as the number-one producer of gyokuro in the country. While he seemed surprised to win, in reality, he could have seen it coming. A third-generation farmer, Kuma-san manages a coveted parcel of land in the misty mountains of Yame. He farms with a winning combination of scientific rigor and intuition, and the nuance and depth of his leaves is truly remarkable.

Zach Mangan: Can you tell me your family's history?

Masahiro Kuma: I am the third generation after my grandfather and father to farm this land. Historically we have been focused on gyokuro since that time, but my father was also a cattle farmer—mainly for beef. After tea production became mechanized, he became a full-time tea farmer. So our history of making tea is roughly seventy years.

Can you talk a little about Joyomachi, where your farm is located?

Joyomachi is actually known for producing some of Fukuoka's most refined and expensive sencha. Though recently, we've developed a reputation for gyokuro [in part due to Masahiro-san's first prize in the gyokuro category of the National Tea Fair]. Hoshinomura is of course the most famous area in Yame, but Joyomachi is emerging as well.

In your opinion, how does Yame gyokuro production differ from Uji's?

It is a different approach—an appreciation of a different profile in each place that drives the technique. Uji has a deep appreciation for an incredibly rich profile, and their fertilization techniques are quite different from ours. I was really surprised. In some places,

the amount of fertilizer they use in one year is equivalent to what we would use in three or four years. But their technique of cultivation is amazing, and their tea is like foie gras. In Yame, our understanding of sencha production has influenced how we shape our gyokuro leaves and the leaf shape of the finished tea now sets the standard in Japan. I think that is something special about Yame.

What is your plan for the future?

In Japan now, the advancement of mechanization in production is allowing the tea industry to expand and grow. Even so, my hope is to focus on quality and remain a small-production farmer even in the future. I just don't feel this large-scale mechanization is suitable for Yame. I think it is better to remain unique and focus on singular products that can't be replicated elsewhere.

What is your desert-island tea?

I would bring tea I could have with meals…so sencha!

Gyokuro fields, Yame, Fukuoka Prefecture

production is a dwindling art that gets more uncommon each year, as many older tea producers retire—it is an art that could be lost someday. Few without a family history of gyokuro farming set out to produce it. And being that gyokuro farming is a rural profession with limited financial prospects, many would-be producers choose not to stay in the family business. In towns around Uji in Kyoto, former gyokuro fields that have gone to seed are a common sight. These farms are becoming monuments to the past. Even so, there has been a shift of interest in gyokuro in Japan, however small, and interest is certainly building in the West.

Gyokuro is a unique style of tea that is grown and processed using a specialized method. It is not a type of tea plant. Rather, the process that the tea undergoes creates its unique profile. The most notable aspect of gyokuro, like with the tencha used to make matcha, is that the tea bushes undergo an intense shading process during the final three weeks prior to harvest. The tea bushes are gradually shaded for longer periods of time until the plants spend twenty-four hours a day in near-total darkness. Gyokuro bushes are grown in a style called shizenshitate, unpruned, and in contrast to orderly sencha they come to resemble small trees. Why are the bushes unpruned? This method allows for the most precious leaves to shoot upward toward the little available light beneath their shaded canopy. It also allows for easier handpicking, as all of the leaves are positioned between waist and hip height when it comes time to harvest.

To that point, the highest-grade gyokuros are harvested by hand. Some high-quality gyokuros are machine harvested, as are almost all lower-grade gyokuros. Unlike sencha, gyokuro is not produced at commercial scale, since it is prohibitively expensive and time-consuming to farm. But the brewed tea, served in thimble-size cups, condenses all the flavors of Japan's storied kaiseki cuisine into one profound, intoxicating sip. Gyokuro is more than tea. It represents not only tradition, but an endless journey of refining, experimenting, and striving for perfection.

GROWING GYOKURO
A Happy Accident
Gyokuro originated in Uji, just south of Kyoto. While gyokuro has many origin stories, it can most likely be traced back to a farming accident.

GYOKURO

FLAVOR PROFILE:
Rich, savory umami. Concentrated sweetness.
Thick, unctuous mouthfeel.

ESTABLISHED PRODUCTION AREAS INCLUDE:
Uji: Shirakawa, Kyotanabe, and Minami Yamashiro
Fukuoka Prefecture: Hoshinomura, Yabemura, Joyomachi, and Kurogi

EMERGING PRODUCTION AREAS INCLUDE:
Shizuoka Prefecture: Okabe

During particularly cold springs, farmers would build covered structures to protect their tea plants from frost. The structures limited sunlight, and farmers likely discovered that their teas, when shaded for longer periods, developed a richer flavor profile. That would not necessarily have been a surprise though. Teas grown on the misty mountainsides of China under diffuse sunlight were known to be especially pungent. And when tea first landed in Kyoto, a great deal of it was grown beneath tall trees that offered ample shade. These teas were prized for their flavor and aroma. In all likelihood, the discovery of gyokuro was a happy accident just the same.

Soil

The outcome of a gyokuro, as with any Japanese tea, depends on the soil. The soil conditions for gyokuro are particularly important. Since gyokuro undergoes several weeks of growth under low-sunlight conditions, it is critical that nutrients from the ground are supplied to the plant in greater abundance. Tea plants naturally thrive in nitrogen-rich soil, and in order to create the intense umami gyokuro is known for, nitrogen-rich fertilizer is applied throughout the year. Even today, most growers follow strict traditional protocols of using natural additives for fertilization.

The most common fertilizers are made from daizukasu, the discarded fiber from soybeans after they are crushed for oil, and fish meal, made up of the bones, meat, and oil from food-grade fish. Each producer has a recipe and does not share it. Fertilization schedules vary, but fertilizer is typically applied during the early fall, winter, and early spring. The question of how best to fertilize makes for a passionate topic of conversation among gyokuro farmers, with Uji and Yame producers sometimes taking divergent paths. Gyokuro producers in Uji especially like to talk about their liberal use of high-cost natural fertilizers with a beaming sense of pride. Years of adjustment and experimentation have allowed them to fine-tune their recipes to complement the soil and micro-regional weather patterns of their fields. I have gathered that Yame farmers use less fertilizer, allowing the shading to imbue their teas with richness. Is there one correct way to fertilize? Of course not—it's these regional differences of approach that make each tea unique. Producing gyokuro is a laborious process that requires a keen understanding of biology, meteorology, and ecology. All steps must be taken to ensure each plant gets the proper nutrients to survive and thrive under very low-light conditions. But when it comes to producing the rich, distilled umami of gyokuro, soil is only one piece of the puzzle. The selection of the cultivar and the style and duration of shading are also of paramount importance.

Shading

The single most important differentiator for gyokuro is the shading process it undergoes. It is absolutely integral to the character of the tea. What do we mean by shading? Gyokuro, like the tencha used to create matcha, undergoes a gradual restriction of sunlight by intentional shading. The tea plants are grown in full sun until the farmer decides it is time to begin shading anywhere from three to five weeks before harvest. The average time of shading is about twenty to twenty-five days. Black synthetic coverings known as kanreisha are used to shade about 99.5 percent of gyokuro. These nets provide consistent and reliable shading and can be stacked to block even more sunlight. They are also reusable, making them cost effective compared to natural shades that degrade over time. The more traditional shades, used in less than .5 percent of gyokuro production, are called honzu. These utilize rice straw scattered over the top of a rattan roof. Honzu shading is reserved for the most expensive gyokuro production each year in places like Yame and Uji. This method is time-consuming and expensive as the shades must be replaced each year. But many say the flavor and aroma of gyokuro shaded with honzu is substantially different. While kanreisha block sunlight in a predictable fashion, honzu shades allow in dappled light in a unique and sometimes unpredictable pattern, allowing Mother Nature to have more of a say in the final product. Additionally, rice straw allows humid air that might get trapped to escape, making for cooler growing conditions, and tea's cellular processes work more slowly at lower temperatures. The slower-growing leaves pull more nutrients from the soil, leading to a higher concentration of flavor and aroma and making for a deeper, richer profile. While some believe honzu shading is superior, I have had revelatory gyokuro produced with kanreisha.

How exactly shading affects the final flavor of gyokuro is complex, but most basically it alters tea plant growth in three major ways. As tea grows it photosynthesizes sunlight and converts amino acids into catechin—a flavonoid more commonly known as an antioxidant. Catechin likely protects the plant from cellular damage caused by intense amounts of direct UV light. When a tea plant is shaded and photosynthesis is slowed, less of its amino acids, especially theanine, are converted into catechin. Amino acids are what account for the rich umami of gyokuro and also help to amplify its sweetness. Catechin has a bitter and astringent quality on the palate, and the low levels found in gyokuro mean the tea is beautifully rich without being bitter. Additionally, during shading the tea plant grows toward whatever little sunlight remains, and its leaves stretch out to increase the surface area available for photosynthesis. This makes each leaf thinner, more delicate, and more pliable. Lastly, without a steady stream of sun, the tea plant begins to produce more of the photosynthesizing chemical chlorophyll to compensate for low-light conditions. This impacts the color of the tea leaf, making for a deep green, almost blue color. The fragrance of gyokuro also develops during the shading process. In Uji especially, a fragrance known as ooika develops when a tea plant is selected, shaded, and fertilized for gyokuro production. Much of Uji gyokuro's ooika comes from elevated levels of dimethyl sulfide, a chemical responsible for the deep oceanic fragrance of nori seaweed. This captivating fragrance is celebrated as a sure sign of the labor that went into crafting this remarkable tea.

Harvest

After shading, the tea leaves are picked. The majority of gyokuros are harvested by machine. This machine, called a sentei ki, is run along the top of the plants and cuts them evenly like a hedge trimmer. This process is efficient, cost effective, and works well.

But the highest grades of gyokuro, many of which we sell at Kettl, are picked by hand in a process called tezumi. Tezumi requires a team of skilled tea professionals with experience picking. Imagine the added expense of increasing your workforce by upwards of ten times. But only experienced hand-harvesters, not machines, can do a near-perfect job. In the tezumi process each individual leaf is seen, considered, and then picked. Hand-picking results in less stem and less thick, mature leaf making it into the final tea.

Left: Gyokuro beneath honzu shading *Right:* Baskets for gathering gyokuro during harvest

Left: Saemidori cultivar *Right:* Tasting tea with a farmer, Fukuoka Prefecture

Once the picking is complete, farmers must race to get the leaves to the factory. As with almost every other category of Japanese green tea, the first step in processing is steaming. The leaves are steamed to halt oxidation and "lock in" the deep-green hue of the shaded leaf. Steaming length for gyokuro generally skews toward the shorter side, putting it in the category of asamushi, or light-steamed tea. This shorter steaming halts oxidation while maintaining as much of the character of the fresh leaf as possible. Lighter steaming also breaks down less of the plant fiber and cellulose, preventing the leaf from breaking up during the rolling process. As a result, the final leaves have a beautiful, needle-like shape.

After steaming, a series of rolling and drying steps are undertaken before the final rolling and shaping of the tea. The final hiire firing process, very popular in Fukuoka Prefecture, is less stylistically appropriate for Uji gyokuro. Uji gyokuro maintains its very fresh, oceanic, and sometimes floral characteristics. To help focus and attenuate the flavors of Uji gyokuro, it is finished with a short-term aging in cold storage known as jukusei. This allows the flavor of the gyokuro to settle and for all of its amino acids and fragrant compounds to find a center—this process is much like resting a soup or stock for a day to intensify its flavors.

Most gyokuro from Yame does not undergo the jukusei process—hiire firing is used instead. This process helps to refine the tea and maintain the fresh, vibrant grassiness Yame gyokuros are known for.

Cultivars

When it comes to gyokuro, several cultivars are common. In Uji, just south of Kyoto, Uji Hikari, Gokou, Uji Midori, Kyoumidori, Samidori, and Saemidori are often used. In the Yame region of Fukuoka Prefecture, Saemidori dominates but new cultivars like Kirari 31 have been making inroads. What is common to all of these cultivars is that they can produce a rich, vibrant umami, have a natural sweetness and pleasant aroma, and have a stable color. Just as wines depend on the grape used, gyokuros' endless expressions depend on the cultivar used in their production. While there are many single-cultivar gyokuros, blending is also common.

BREWING GYOKURO

The prospect of brewing gyokuro can strike fear in the hearts of tea drinkers, as the process has a reputation for being a bit tricky. But after a few tries, it becomes a fun and intuitive process. The main point to remember is that gyokuro uses a ratio of less water to tea leaf, a lower brew temperature, and a longer brew time.

In order to enhance the umami profile of the gyokuro, cooler water is used in brewing—generally around 120–140°F. To make up for the lower temperature, more tea leaf and a longer steep time (about two minutes) is employed. When brewing high-quality gyokuro, very little water can be used to achieve a rich, sweet tea. Generally I start with a ratio of about 12 milliliters (.4 fl. oz.) of water per 1 gram of leaf. So for a 5 gram serving of tea, I use about 60 milliliters (2 fl. oz.) of water. This is a great starting point. But each tea is unique and has its own ideal profile, which requires a little bit of searching to bring out. That being said, most gyokuro should taste great within these parameters. If it is overly bitter, add a bit more water to find the sweet spot. You can also try using room temperature or cold water for an even longer brew. This will exemplify the richness of the gyokuro while reducing the chance of astringency to almost zero.

GYOKURO BREWING INSTRUCTIONS

1. Boil the water.
2. Pour 60 mL (2 fl. oz.) of hot water into your empty teapot
    and allow the water to sit for two minutes.
3. Pour the water from the teapot into an empty teacup.
4. Add 5–7 g tea to your warmed teapot. If the quality
    of your gyokuro is high, you can use slightly more leaf.
5. You can pour the water between the cup and a yuzamashi
    (a spouted cooling vessel) or another cup until it reaches
    a temperature of about 120–140°F (60°C).
6. Pour the water into the teapot and brew for two minutes.
7. After two minutes, pour the tea slowly. You can shake the
    teapot gently to allow the last remaining drops to fall into
    your cup.
8. Enjoy. You can rebrew gyokuro three to four times.
    Increase the temperature of the water slightly for
    subsequent brews.

BUYING GYOKURO

When buying gyokuro in a shop, always request as much information as possible about the tea. Try to learn its prefecture and region of origin and, if possible, the grower's name. More information and transparency means you can be sure you are buying from a reputable seller. Packaging should be opaque—not clear glass—and free of oxygen.

STORING GYOKURO

At Kettl, we recommend keeping unopened gyokuro refrigerated. Once opened, portion out an amount that makes sense—maybe a week's worth—and repack the rest and return to the fridge.

CHAPTER SEVEN

Bancha, Houjicha, Genmaicha

BANCHA REMAINS PERHAPS THE MOST WIDELY CONSUMED TEA within the Japanese archipelago. Bancha refers to teas from the later harvests. Earlier chapters discussed shincha, the new crop, and ichiban sencha—both teas that are produced from the first harvest. Gyokuro and tencha come from this first picking as well. But after the first picking, the tea plant continues to grow and produces a second flush of leaves known as nibancha. Nibancha makes up the majority of green tea sold in supermarkets in Japan and almost the entire bulk of what is sold at large retailers and small tea shops abroad. Nibancha is harvested in mid-to-late June. And a third harvest, referred to as sanbancha, or often just bancha, follows and is picked in July or August. With each picking, the leaves become more mature and mellow in flavor and aroma. Bancha tea produces a soft, gentle flavor with a much lower caffeine content and higher levels of natural vitamin C. It is a great choice for those that want to drink tea throughout the day without fear of consuming too much caffeine.

While bancha can be had on its own, more often it serves as the base for other types of Japanese green tea including both genmaicha and houjicha. *(continued on p. 132)*

HIROKAZU SUGIURA, RYUOUEN CHAHO

Founded in 1875, Ryuouen Chaho continues to be regarded as one of Kyoto's most esteemed tea sellers. While the majority of the shop's sales can be attributed to its matcha, to those who know their houjicha, Ryuouen is thought to offer some of the best in Japan. I had a chance to discuss some of the finer points of houjicha production with Hirokazu Sugiura, the future head of Ryuouen. Sugiura-san oversees all points of the family business with a particular love for tea production and manufacturing.

Zach Mangan: What makes your houjicha so unique?

Hirokazu Sugiura: This might sound a bit antiquated, but for us the most important thing is the mind we put in. That's the mind to do business with honesty. Rather than selling what's cheap at a high price or adding sloppy changes to the products we sell, we want to sell what's really good at an appropriate price.

In addition to maintaining standards, what is it about your houjicha that is so special?

Without divulging too many secrets [laughs], I can tell you this: We start with great materials and we roast them slowly [so as] not to damage the ingredients. It takes more time and we can't make a large amount. If you roast it strongly, the leaves pop like a popcorn. They are puffed up as the water is reduced and the volume increases, but the taste of the ingredient can disappear a little bit. This is how we maintain the rich umami of our houjicha.

So you roast each tea specifically to accentuate its inherent flavor? Sounds just like specialty coffee.

Correct. Teas that are more mature require longer roasting to balance aroma, where teas from the first flush require less time leaving more of the fresh taste of spring intact.

Ryuouen Chaho matcha tins, Kyoto

And you recommend a shorter brew time for your high-grade houjicha?

That's right. With hot water, even just ten to twenty seconds is all you need to draw out a wonderful aromas with no bitterness.

Thanks so much for your time. My last question: What is your desert-island tea?

It might be strange that I don't recommend houjicha even though I'm selling it. But originally Kyoto was known for matcha. And the tea ceremony is an important part of our history. So I would take matcha.

HOUJICHA

A classic style of tea that comes, more often than not, from bancha is houjicha. Generally speaking, houjicha is made from the green leaves and stems of later-harvest bancha. Bancha contains less caffeine, theanine, and polyphenols—all the flavor components that make great sencha. Due to the lack of these compounds, bancha is roasted, a process that imparts a new layer of flavor. Generally, houjicha is a green tea whose aroma really trumps flavor. The satisfying toastiness can be reminiscent of coffee, toasted nuts, chestnuts, and even caramelized sugar. Intensely satisfying to say the least.

Houjicha is so ubiquitous that it is sometimes just referred to as ocha, or tea. Traditionally, houjicha came only from bancha and was roasted heavily. These traditional-style houjichas can be found in the backstreets of Tokyo or the markets of Kyoto—the unmistakable aroma of roasted tea will draw you in from blocks away.

Left, Roasted kukicha *Right,* Unroasted kukicha

BANCHA

FLAVOR PROFILE:
Houjicha: Toasted, caramelized, and easy drinking.
Genmaicha: Nutty, toasted, refreshing.

ESTABLISHED PRODUCTION AREAS INCLUDE:
All major tea-producing regions of Japan

Today, houjicha is consumed in every prefecture in Japan and is manufactured in every prefecture that produces tea. This means there are wonderful varieties of houjicha with subtle differences to be sampled wherever you go; like the regional amaros of Italy, each reflects the taste of the place where it is produced.

In addition, a more contemporary style of houjicha has emerged with a lighter roast profile that accentuates and draws out more of the inherent qualities of the leaf, much in the way lighter-roast coffees showcase the natural profile of the bean rather than masking it with too deep a roast. These newer styles of houjicha often utilize the first harvest of tea, which can be difficult to roast due to an array of aromatic compounds this product contains that don't always translate well when roasted. The work-around is to use primarily the stem instead of the leaves when roasting first-flush tea—which creates bocha (stick tea), kukicha houjicha (roasted stems removed from sencha), or karigane houjicha (roasted stems of shaded tea). As mentioned, these lighter-roast stem teas are a relatively new style and accentuate a new characteristic—umami as well as fragrance.

Left: Unroasted stem *Right:* Roasted stem

MANUFACTURE

Up until roasting, houjicha goes through the same steps as other green teas by way of aracha (unrefined tea) processing. With traditional houjicha, after the late-harvest tea has been picked and processed it is ready for the secondary process of roasting. So just to be clear: the tea leaves are roasted after being steamed, rolled, dried, and shaped. In regards to kukicha or stem-based light-roast houjicha, the stems are removed during primary processing, then collected and roasted. The roasting process varies based on region, but generally, a hojiki—a metal drum that rotates while being heated by gas—is used. As the drum rotates, the tea leaves are heated and eventually roasted. The exact temperature and duration of the roasting process are often closely guarded secrets. Apart from the inherent qualities of the tea that's being roasted, the small nuances of this process are what distinguishes one brand's houjicha from another. The plant sugars undergo caramelization, in a process known as the Maillard reaction, when the internal temperature of the leaf rises above 280°F (140°C). The range of roasting temperatures is generally 280–320°F. The duration can be anywhere from five to twenty minutes depending on the style of the tea. In certain areas, ceramic beads are added to the roasting drum. As the ceramic heats up it produces a broad range of far infrared radiation. The full spectrum heat can penetrate the tea leaf and add an additional intensity to the roast—and therefore a more intense flavor. Some traditional tea makers may also use charcoal, which produces a similar outcome. But by and large, charcoal is quite rare these days.

GENMAICHA

Genmaicha is a tea that many westerners are familiar with and have encountered in sushi restaurants. It is often referred to as "brown rice tea." In fact, genmai (玄米) means brown rice in Japanese. Genmaicha is generally a bancha blended with toasted brown rice. The ratio is between 30 to 50 percent rice to tea leaf. The brown rice adds a refreshing, nutty aroma to the mellow flavor of the bancha. And when it is brewed and served hot the aroma of the rice is further enhanced. Genmaicha works well with a variety of foods and is often served in sushi restaurants as it can refresh the palate between pieces of fish. Genmaicha is also well suited for serving with sweets and pairs well with baked and toasted flavors. One of my first memories of Japanese tea is a cup of hot genmaicha with a piece of dark chocolate. It was a distinctly wonderful pairing.

Genmaicha, sencha leaves blended with roasted brown rice

Genmaicha

THE ROOTS OF GENMAICHA

Why was brown rice first mixed with tea leaves? Genmaicha has its roots in rural Japan. The lore is that when harvests were lean and less tea was available, roasted brown rice was blended with tea leaves at a roughly 50–50 ratio, doubling the amount of tea that would have to last between harvests. Additionally, the brown rice added some needed nutrition at times when food was scarce. But as food security improved in Japan, genmaicha's popularity continued. The harmony of flavors in this countryside tea caught on, and genmaicha gained popularity in city centers as well. It has become a tea drunk throughout Japan and is now produced in some form in almost every prefecture that manufactures tea.

GENMAIMATCHA

A current trend, and one we love at Kettl, is blending the genmaicha with a small amount of matcha powder. This adds a wonderful sweetness and a more pronounced mouthfeel to the tea. It is the ultimate food-pairing tea and is in our cups most days before, during, and after lunch.

Houjicha

BREWING GENMAICHA

Genmaicha is a hearty tea and can withstand hotter temperatures. In fact, if you love the rice flavor of genmai, using hotter water will bring it to the fore. Using slightly cooler water will pull out more of the green tea aroma and flavor.

BREWING HOUJICHA

Like genmaicha, houjicha is a sturdy tea that can withstand higher water temperatures, actually benefiting from them. Houjicha, being roasted, contains less catechin and caffeine—compounds that can lead to a bitter brew—and high temperatures help to pull out houjicha's enchanting toasty aroma.

STORING BANCHA

Bancha benefits less from being refrigerated, so keeping it in an opaque airtight container at room temperature is best. Once opened, we recommend drinking bancha within three months.

Part Three

THE

CRAFT:

FROM

PROCURING

TO

TASTE

—

Tea evaluation, Shizuoka

CHAPTER EIGHT

The Taste of Japanese Tea

I REALIZED RECENTLY THAT I CAN QUICKLY AND PRETTY accurately explain the difference between light-steamed and deep-steamed sencha. It's not too difficult to express to a customer what they should expect in terms of profile when it comes to matcha from Fukuoka versus matcha from Uji. And explaining how roast level affects the caffeine in houjicha is something that can be achieved in under a minute. But there is one question I get often that is worthy of further exploration: *What does green tea taste like?*

AN ENDLESS SPECTRUM OF PROFILES

The job of describing the taste of green tea may seem straightforward, but it is challenging. Try to answer this: What does an apple taste like? Like an apple, of course. But almost everyone has some experience with an apple and can imagine pretty quickly what general flavor, aroma, and texture they might expect. With green tea the pool of experience is smaller and the vernacular to describe it dwindles pretty quickly when reached for. Overwhelmingly, the adjective used to describe tea is *earthy*. As in from the earth. The planet. Something carbon based. This is about as broad a term imaginable and speaks to the fact that we have a lot of

room for parsing out the finer points of a tea's profile and translating it into terms we can actually use. And how do we do this? The answer is simple: Drink more green tea and consume more of everything that we can use as a flavor reference, such as fruit, spices, vegetables, etc.

Wine and coffee both present great points of comparison when thinking about how to "build your palate" when it comes to tea. Tim Gaiser, a master sommelier, outlines on his site how he tastes wine using the "deductive tasting technique," which can be used to pinpoint a wine's grape variety, origin, and even vintage. While this level of evaluation certainly is not necessary for the simple enjoyment of tea, it does show you that like most things, the ability to really taste and describe the flavor of wine—or tea, coffee, or just about anything else—can be learned with practice. Our palate is like a muscle: the more we use it, the stronger it becomes. But a simple explanation of the exercises can be helpful in getting started.

THE FIVE DISTINCT TASTES OF GREEN TEA

When taste and aroma combine, we have flavor. In reality, much of what we are "tasting" when we drink tea is a combination of taste, which is experienced on your tongue, and aroma, which is decoded by your nose. Japanese green tea has thousands of variations in aroma but if we close our nose and take a sip, we have only five categories of taste: sweetness, saltiness, sourness, bitterness—and umami, which loosely translates to "savoriness."

While identifying the five categories of taste may seem straightforward, it can be complex to establish the degree to which each taste category is present in a particular tea. When thinking about sweetness, the Saemidori cultivar comes to mind. For saltiness, some kabuse shaded teas have a distinct saline quality reminiscent of the sea. If thinking about sourness, then goishicha, a fermented bancha from Shikoku, fits the bill, with its sour-plum-like tang. For bitterness, light-steamed sencha from either Uji or Shizuoka often have a distinct, elegant bitter note.

And if what we are looking for is an example of umami, then look no further than gyokuro, with its textbook brothy notes that summarize exactly what the umami experience is all about.

BUILDING YOUR PALATE

So how does any of the above help to answer the question: *What does green tea taste like?* Well, before we can say, we must establish a breadth of experience of flavor and aroma to draw from. Something I call *flavor memory*. People will always describe flavors and aromas by drawing comparisons to things that are personal to them. The more experiences one has to draw from, the easier it is to express oneself. It's a personal vocabulary: the more words you know, the easier it is to describe your experience of flavor. And food isn't the only possible reference. Aromatic experiences often live vividly in your memory and can be triggered by the taste of teas. It can be a bit awkward at first to express yourself using memories of tastes and scents, but the more you do it, the easier and more helpful it becomes.

Japanese tea, for example, is often compared to spinach. Most people have a lot of direct experience eating spinach and therefore it's an easy reference to make. And while yes, green tea does share some of the green, chlorophyll flavors of spinach—what about going deeper? How about sorrel, arugula, or mustard greens? As we become more confident in our palate and how to express what we're tasting, it becomes a rewarding and fun experience to parse out the tapestry of flavors and aromas in tea.

As a fun exercise at Kettl, we love to set up sessions where we taste spices, herbs, and fruits, just to become familiar with the range of flavors that are out there to be tasted. Recently, upon eating a husk cherry I was delighted to discover that its acidic, tropical flavor reminded me of a note I often pick up in sencha from Kagoshima. I discovered a new point of reference for describing tea and created a strong flavor memory that will be with me forever, all while having fun.

FIVE TASTES, MULTIPLE AROMAS

When we describe a tea using taste in combination with aroma, the possibilities become endless. This approach offers a much deeper vocabulary to express the subtleties of tea and encourages us to access our flavor memory—all of the collected flavor experiences we have accumulated

Upper Left: Tasting several single-cultivar matchas.
Lower left: Sencha *Right:* Gyokuro

over our lives. Using our experiences can help us describe tea with more freedom. For example, the following description is a comparison of two matchas from Uji, both from the same cultivar:

Matcha A: Sweet grass (aroma from my childhood), cashew (a flavor I am accustomed to), green straw (tatami, an aroma I first experienced in Japan).

Matcha B: Nori seaweed (a flavor I know from eating sushi), raspberry (a flavor I am accustomed to), tomato-vine flowers (an aroma I remember from my mother's garden).

The aromas are so different while the teas have so much in common. They share a style of tea (matcha), an origin (Uji), and cultivar (Asahi). On paper, they seem to be the same. But of course, like with wine, the microterroir and the point of view and skill of the farmer have an incredible impact on the final flavor and aroma of the teas.

One palate exercise we love is this: brew two teas side by side and taste. Make sure to note what flavors, aromas, and textures you pick out in each. Taste them when they are hot, when they have begun to cool, and when they have cooled. Notes you didn't notice when a tea was hot might become more apparent once it cools a bit. This is a simple exercise but it can be truly challenging. Use your creativity and write down whatever it is that you experience, even if it seems strange (wet basement, fresh mowed lawn, red Skittle). There are no wrong answers.

SUMMARY

The palate is a muscle that needs to be strengthened. The more experience you have tasting and describing tea, the easier it will become. Grab a notebook and jot down at least five things you taste every time you drink your green tea for a week and see how your palate changes in that time. A note: while wines have a highly developed list of flavors and aromas that are referenced around the world, Japanese tea does not. So depending where you are from, you may build a set of flavor references that differs from someone living somewhere else. Perhaps sencha might remind you of nori seaweed if you are from Korea or Japan, or of spinach if you grew up in Cleveland. Our palates are personal, and everyone will taste something different.

To that point, drinking tea with others in a group can also be enlightening. You might be surprised by what someone with a different palate notices. And before long, you might be picking up on their notes, too. Most importantly, don't forget to have fun and enjoy the journey! Learning and enjoying oneself are often two sides of the same coin.

CHAPTER NINE

Teapots Demystified

THE CERAMIC TRADITIONS OF JAPAN ARE DEEP, AND THERE are many different styles and materials used in traditional Japanese teapots. While shapes, sizes, and colors may differ, most Japanese teapots are made from clay. Clay is the ideal material for a teapot. Clay is renewable, sturdy, light, and can tolerate very high-temperature water. Clay is also porous, so the inside of clay teapots develop a patina. Over time this patina can positively impact the flavor of brewed tea, adding depth and tempering bitter or astringent flavors.

While many teapots are intricately designed, the majority of Japanese tea ware is not overly ornamental. Function is the key, and Japanese teapots are meant to be used daily. Japanese design philosophy, heavily influenced by Japan's mingei folk- and craft-art movement of the 1920s, values objects that are a joy to use day in, day out. The Japanese teapot, or kyusu, is exactly such an object. A kyusu craftsperson will always ask of a quality teapot: Is it easy to handle? Does the tea pour well? Is it balanced in your hand when you use it? If even only those three questions are met with a "yes," the teapot can be considered a success. Of course, truly exquisite teapots will meet those criteria and still offer more—balancing beauty, simplicity, and functionality. When I asked the master teapot maker Seiji Ito what makes a great teapot, *(continued on p. 152)*

SEIJI ITO (JINSHU)

Seiji Ito is a celebrated potter from Tokoname who has been making kyusu (traditional Japanese teapots), teacups, vases, and other ceramics for over fifty years. Ito-san, who makes work under the name Jinshu, is perhaps one of the most respected and celebrated contemporary teapot makers in Japan. His work is equal parts tradition, peerless perfection, and curious exploration. Ito-san has won many awards including the title "master traditional craftsman" bestowed by the Japanese minister of trade and economy.

I sat with him at his studio in Tokoname on a hot summer day to gain some insight into the city and learn more about his creative approach to making tools for everyday life.

Zach Mangan: Can you tell me a bit about your personal history?

Seiji Ito: Well, my father was a potter from very early on in his life. After I quit my first job, I followed him and became a potter. That was when I was twenty and I am sixty-eight now, so almost fifty years ago.

So, your family has a history of pottery?

My father grew up near a pottery shop and started helping there part-time when he was a kid. It was just a natural thing how he began to do it.

Did you receive any formal training?

I learned the technique of the potter's wheel by studying with my father…or maybe observing is the right word. But he didn't make kyusus like what I imagined. So I began experimenting on my own.

Just through self-study?

Well, in this area, there are many samples to learn from. I started by asking people a little bit about the important points for production and actually doing it. If I think about it now, my kyusu is not especially "Tokoname-like" in a way. I think my kyusu sits a bit outside the traditional style—something relatively more handmade-like. A bit different from the traditional style.

Ito-san and his wife, Mieko Ito

In your opinion, what is most important about the design of a good kyusu?

Basically, a kyusu is a tool to brew tea. So first and foremost, it is important that delicious tea can be brewed with it. And being that it is a tool, it has to be easy to use. This is why I craft my kyusu with wider lids.

I know wider kyusus let the tea leaves spread out, meaning more uniform contact with water. Is that why?

Yes, and because it is easier to put tea in and take the old tea out of a kyusu with a relatively larger lid. The traditionally round-shaped kyusus all seem to have smaller lids. For me, I think usability is the most important thing.

Is there anything else that you absolutely cannot compromise on in terms of design?

The spout must prevent dripping!

he answered matter-of-factly: "It has to be easy to use." When I asked if a good kyusu has any other essential qualities, he answered: "The spout must prevent dripping!" Japanese teapots are truly tools. And as with any tool, once you've used a good one, it's hard to imagine getting the job done without it.

FREQUENTLY ASKED QUESTIONS

I receive several emails a week from customers who want to know more about Kettl's Japanese teapots. There seems to be a lot of uncertainty about what pot works best for what tea—and what to avoid when using or handling these unique tea wares.

I thought it might be helpful to compile answers to some of the most common questions I get asked. What follows is a handy reference for those shopping for a new Japanese teapot or for those who already own one and have questions about care. Making great Japanese tea requires a great teapot. Whether you are just getting into Japanese tea or are already an aficionado, you can get the most out of your teas by brewing with the right equipment.

What are those side-handled pots?

These are our kyusu—the famous side-handled teapots used throughout Japan. While Japan has a storied tradition of creating world-class teapots in a variety of shapes and styles, the side-handled pot is the most quintessential and classic Japanese design. The handle on a kyusu is generally hollow and is positioned at a slight angle to allow for unencumbered pouring and ergonomic use. After trying it, it just feels natural.

Where is Tokoname, and why are so many Japanese teapots made there?

Tokoname, a small town in Aichi Prefecture, produces the majority of Japanese teapots—many in the orange-ish iron-rich clay of the area. Tokoname has a rich history of ceramics that dates back to the Heian period (794–1185). Even from this early period, Tokoname produced an immense amount of pottery, eclipsing many of the older more established pottery towns. But it wasn't until during the late Edo period into the Meiji period that Tokoname tea ware became popular. According to Seiji Ito, "While it feels like a deep, long tradition, Tokoname kyusu are

Ceramicists at the studio of Gyoko in Tokoname, Aichi Prefecture

still pretty young in the grand scheme of things." He adds, "Even now, things are changing and developing around Tokoname kyusus."

Today, Tokoname is the teapot capital of Japan, known for its shudei style of clay, which is a bright reddish-orange due to its high levels of iron. The majority of the kyusu made in Tokoname are unglazed and fired only in electric kilns. Balance and precision are the defining characteristics of teapots from this region. To the untrained eye, it can seem inconceivable that these perfectly crafted teapots could be made by hand. In fact, the highest-caliber kyusu are indeed 100 percent handcrafted.

Japanese teapots seem kind of small. Why is that?

Japanese teapots can range in size, but the most popular hold about 150–266 milliliters (5–9 fl. oz.) of water. A serving of tea in Japan is often smaller than the mug-sized servings we are used to in the West, and smaller pots allow for a level of balance and control that can be difficult to attain in a heavy teapot. So, keeping the pot size a bit smaller means an easier pour. Also, Japanese tea can be re-brewed; making several smaller servings and savoring the flavor is a wonderful way to experience tea. I generally drink between 180–250 milliliters (6–9 fl. oz.) of tea in a single sitting, so I love a kyusu in the 250–266 milliliters (9–10 fl. oz.) range. And for gyokuro, I like a smaller 120 milliliters (4 fl. oz.) kyusu.

Can I use my teapot to brew any kind of tea?

Japanese teapots made from unglazed clay are mildly porous and can absorb flavors and aromas from the tea brewed in them. Because of that, it is a good idea to stick to one style of tea for each teapot. The main thing to avoid is brewing flavored or scented teas like jasmine or herbal blends in a pot you use for high-quality green tea. The fragrance can be absorbed by the kyusu and stick around long after you've cleaned it. Soon enough your sencha or houjicha will have notes of jasmine—not a great combination in my opinion.

What do you recommend for brewing gyokuro?

The serving-size of gyokuro (often to people's surprise) is much smaller than that of other Japanese teas. A single serving can range from 30–90 milliliters (1–3 fl. oz.). Because of that, smaller, more delicate teapots are often used. While you can make gyokuro in a normal sized kyusu, it is a nice ritual to have a separate piece that you can bring out to brew the good stuff. In addition to a small kyusu, another popular implement for brewing gyokuro is a shiboridashi. A shiboridashi functions almost exactly like a Chinese gaiwan and is more or less a small bowl with a spout and a lid that catches the leaves. No filter is involved. This style of teapot really only works with light-steamed, larger-leaf teas and does require some getting used to. But once you have the hang of it, it is a

meditative vessel and is such a pleasure to use. When it comes to brewing gyokuro, what matters is that you find something you really connect with and then use it every day.

Can I put my teapot on the stove?

No, you can't. Japanese ceramic teapots are meant to brew tea, not boil water. If heated directly, they will crack. If you need to put a Japanese teapot on the stove, use a tetsubin. Tetsubin are cast-iron kettles that are meant to be heated over charcoal, electric burners, or indirect flame. True tetsubin generally hold a liter or more of water and differ from the small (often made in China) cast-iron teapots with removable brew baskets. The inside of a tetsubin is almost always raw with no sealant, whereas the small cast-iron brewing teapots that you commonly see have a shiny lacquer applied. Water boiled in a true tetsubin has a positive impact on the flavor of tea. But while tetsubin may be ideal for boiling water, we do not recommend them for brewing tea, as they tend to hold too much heat.

How should I clean my Japanese teapot?

Ceramic Japanese teapots require nothing more than hot water and your hands for cleaning. We recommend rinsing out your leaves when you are finished (try to avoid leaving wet leaves sitting in the pot overnight). Rinse your teapot well with warm water and use your hand to remove any small particles of leaf that may be hiding in there. Teapots with wider lids are easier to clean—so keep that in mind. If you find that your strainer is blocked with leaf particles, use a water pick (a water flosser for your teeth) or toothpick to carefully unclog it. Always rest your kyusu upside down on a towel with the lid off to dry it.

Ok, I'm ready to buy a Japanese teapot. What should I look for exactly?

When picking a teapot, I think it is important to look for something that you are personally drawn to. It is a tool you will use daily, and it is important that the look and feel of it brings you joy. It is also important that you understand your needs in terms of serving size. Remember that a serving of tea in Japan is often smaller than what we're used to in the West—but finding something that meets your expectations is important. If you are shopping in Japan, be advised that you shouldn't touch a teapot in a shop unless you have asked or it has been offered to you. When handling a teapot, always use two hands and hold the pot low over a table or surface. Feeling how the lid fits will always give you a good idea about the general quality of a teapot. A nice, tight fit with little lateral wiggle is best. Inside, you might find one of many different types of strainers. A top-quality kyusu will have a ceramic strainer in front of the inner spout hole. Since this style of pot has no removable strainer, tea made in it must be brewed and quickly served so that the leaves are not over-brewed. Some less expensive kyusu will have

removable, stainless mesh strainers. In these pots the tea can be brewed and served little by little after the strainer is removed. Finding the style that works for you is best, but brewing and pouring all at once ensures that you enjoy your tea at its optimal temperature. Part of the appeal of teapots is their collectability: there is nothing wrong with a having a few pots for different teas, with different serving sizes and to suit your mood and any occasion.

Discover a pot that you love to use and use it daily. A good kyusu will give you years of happiness and service.

I broke my teapot. What should I do?

Unfortunately, this is a question that we get asked often. Sometimes a lid or spout chips or breaks, and a customer is unsure what to do. First of all, handmade teapots are one of a kind, so ordering a replacement lid is not possible. While gluing a teapot is not a good idea, a technique called kintsugi is suitable for repairing ceramic teaware. Kintsugi uses lacquer combined with gold to safely and effectively reconnect broken pieces of clay. Kintsugi adds a layer of visual depth to teaware and even adds value in the case of certain collectable pieces. But most importantly it is food safe and lasts forever. Finding an artisan capable of repairing your piece using kintsugi will likely be tough if you do not live in a large city, but a quick online search can connect you with an artisan that can help. There are also at-home kits, a more cost-effective solution. Pottery breaks; and if it's any consolation, there's a saying in Japan that when you break a piece of pottery, the pot took a blow that was headed for you. So, while it is never easy to break something, rest easy knowing your piece was only protecting you.

In summary, teapots are a fascinating and useful tool for the Japanese-tea lover. Take your time to research the pot you are looking at. Find something that speaks to you and something you can imagine using daily. And if you make tea every day, make sure you buy a pot that's easy for you to use. Once you select one, enjoy it and use it as often as you can. The more you use it, the better it will become.

CHAPTER TEN

Tea on Ice

PERHAPS ONE OF THE MOST EXCITING ASPECTS OF TEA IS ITS potential to be served cold, or even used as a base for a cocktail. Almost everyone has had iced tea in one form or another, but often the tea used is nothing more than black-tea dust in a bag or a sweetened, syrupy concentrate. When tea is thoughtfully crafted with the intention of being served cold, a new world of flavor possibilities comes to life.

Perhaps the idea of iced tea seems tired or unexciting. I understand completely. It wasn't until I visited a tea shop in Japan and was introduced to high-quality cold-brew tea that I truly understood the range of flavors and aromas that can be expressed in iced tea. In this chapter I will guide you through the process of cold brewing called mizudashi—an approach that uses cold water and a longer brew time that is particular to Japan. I believe this way of brewing can open up new possibilities of flavor and a deeper, richer experience.

Tea served cold or blended can express a set of flavors or aromas you might not experience with hot tea. And tea served in stemware can highlight the possibility of a new tactile relationship to tea. When I help restaurants imagine what their tea program could look like, I often stress the potential for serving teas chilled in a wine glass. Offering hot

tea instead of alcohol to guests who don't drink misses a major point. Certain dining experiences come with drinking wine: having a bottle presented; swirling and clinking glasses; holding stemware while chatting. A guest with a teacup will miss all of that. When presented with tea in a wine glass, the guest who refrains from alcohol can still partake in the ritual of drinking. This is a powerful way that restaurateurs or hosts can make their guests feel at home in the course of sharing a meal. And I should mention, the flavor experience of chilled tea in a wine glass can be as unique and captivating as that of an old Mosel riesling or pinot from Burgundy.

For those who do drink alcohol, tea serves as a striking base to build a cocktail on. The tea plant contains hundreds if not thousands of volatile compounds that can add fragrance, flavor, and texture to a drink. In the chapter ahead I share several of my favorite preparations of cold tea and a couple of cocktail recipes from my good friends.

COLD BREWING TEA

Traditionally, iced tea has been made by brewing tea leaves with hot water and then cooling the brewed tea over ice, a method that makes tea with a similar flavor profile to traditional hot tea.

When hot water reacts with the dry leaf, the high temperature naturally releases many of the tannins, as well as the caffeine, catechin, and many of the aromatic compounds. Tannins, caffeine, and catechins are responsible for the "dry" or slightly bitter taste sometimes present in hot tea. Cold brewing is referred to as mizudashi in Japanese. It is a unique style in which green tea is brewed with cold water over a longer period of time using slightly more leaf. Brewing tea with cold water pulls out the sweeter notes while diminishing most, if not all, of the tea's astringency. The lowered astringency is due to the fact that cold water pulls less tannins and caffeine from the tea but leaves all of the tea's umami and sweetness, making it sweeter and more mild. The longer steep time, up to twelve hours for some teas, compensates for the naturally more

mild-tasting brew and makes green tea with more body and a rich flavor and aroma.

Cold brewing is not only refreshing but also gives you a chance to taste a different flavor profile of a green tea that you may be used to drinking hot.

At Kettl, we think that cold brewing highlights the "fundamental flavor" of a tea. What does that mean? It means you taste the leaf in a state closer to how it would taste in the field. When cold brewed, many green teas will reveal heightened aromas that would otherwise be masked by stronger flavors released in hot water.

Cold brewing tea is simple. I like to use a glass pitcher that holds one or two liters of water.

Recipe

COLD BREWING "MIZUDASHI STYLE"

WHAT YOU WILL NEED:

1 carafe

1–2 L cold, filtered water

10 g sencha, gyokuro, or kabuse tea (loose-leaf)

DIRECTIONS

1. Add about 10 g of loose green tea to your carafe per liter of tea you will brew (1.1 g of tea per 30 mL / 4 fl. oz. water). This may seem like a lot, but remember, you're using much more water than you would to brew hot tea.

2. Fill your carafe with cold, filtered water.

3. Place your carafe in the refrigerator, making sure to cover it so your tea does not absorb any unwanted odors.

4. Let steep. Steep time will vary depending on the type of green tea you are using, the style of the leaf (open, rolled, etc.), and your personal taste. I generally brew 10–12 g of tea in 1 L water for about twelve hours.

5. Stir occasionally with a wooden spoon. Agitating the leaves will help release the tea's flavor and color. How do you know when the tea is done? I taste test along the way and keep an eye on the depth of color; the darker the color, the stronger the brew.

6. Once the tea is steeped to your liking, give it a final stir. After the leaves have settled you can pour the brewed green tea through a sieve and into your serving container. Voila! The best iced green tea you've ever had.

Recipe

COLD BREWING "SHAKEN STYLE"

If you need cold brew in a shorter time frame, we recommend "shaken style" cold tea. We use our Sencha Jou or gyokuro tea bag for this. Our sencha and gyokuro tea bags are filled with 5 grams of premium tea and a touch of matcha powder for added color. We purposely cut the leaf 40 percent smaller, making it easy to brew quickly and with a deep, rich flavor. Shaken cold brew is a delicious treat that you can whip up after a run or a workout, or at the office.

WHAT YOU WILL NEED
1 Sencha Jou tea bag
One 12 fl. oz. thermos or a cocktail shaker
(we recommend our Kinto Shaker)
4 ice cubes
1 glass

DIRECTIONS
1. Place 1 Sencha Jou tea bag in your tumbler and add 4 ice cubes. Whenever possible, try to use filtered water for your ice. The ice will melt and impact the flavor of the tea, so the tastier the water you use for your ice, the tastier your tea will be.
2. Fill a 12 fl. oz. thermos or tumbler 80 percent full with cold filtered water (about 275 mL / 9.5 fl. oz.).
3. Shake vigorously for forty-five seconds. Use all your might and really let it rip. You will hear the ice clinking at first but as you keep shaking the majority of the ice should melt.
4. Pour the shaken tea over ice or you can keep it in your thermos and drink on the go.

Recipe

ICED HOUJICHA

WHAT YOU WILL NEED:
Houjicha
Freshly boiled water
Ice
1 liter glass carafe

DIRECTIONS
1. Fill a 1 L glass carafe with ice.
2. Measure 10 g of houjicha leaf into a teapot.
3. Pour 350 mL (12 fl. oz.) freshly boiled water over the houjicha.
4. Brew for one minute.
5. Pour the brewed houjicha over the ice.
6. Stir and enjoy.

BREWING WITH HOT WATER AND ICE

When using teas with less umami and an intense aroma, like black tea or houjicha, consider brewing the tea hot and then pouring it over ice. This method is sometimes referred to as "flash brewing." It's great for pulling out the roasted and nutty notes of houjicha and produces a refreshing, malty iced black tea.

ICED MATCHA DRINKS

People often request the recipes for our iced matcha and iced matcha oat-milk latte. Both are incredibly satisfying in hot weather—but we find ourselves drinking them throughout the year.

Recipe

ICED MATCHA

When making a cold matcha straight, we recommend shaking the tea. This creates a fine crema and introduces air into the matcha, making for a creamy, decadent drink without any milk.

WHAT YOU WILL NEED:
2 g of sifted matcha
200 mL (7 fl. oz.) cold filtered water
Thermos or cocktail shaker
Ice

DIRECTIONS
1. Add 2 g of sifted matcha powder to your thermos or tumbler.
2. Add 200 mL (7 fl. oz.) of cold filtered water. Screw on the cap tightly and shake vigorously for about 30 seconds. It is important that there is a bit of space at the top of the thermos to allow the matcha and water to move freely.
3. Pour over ice and enjoy. Please note that matcha is a suspension. After a period of time the powder will settle at the bottom of your glass. Drink iced matcha relatively quickly.

Recipe

ICED MATCHA LATTE

For our iced matcha latte, we employ a slightly different technique. We whisk the matcha with hot water, add milk, and then pour over ice. Using 4 grams of matcha means we really need to be certain the tea has completely dissolved—so starting with hot water is best. We do not sweeten our latte; if you choose to do so, add your desired sweetener to the matcha prior to combining it with milk.

DIRECTIONS

1. Warm 220 mL (7.5 fl. oz.) milk or milk alternative in a pot. If you have a steam wand, measure out cold milk and reserve for step 4.
2. Sift 4 g of matcha powder into a bowl, or even better, a spouted bowl.
3. Add 40–50 mL (1.4–1.7 fl. oz.) hot filtered water to the tea. Whisk the matcha until a fine foam appears, about twenty to thirty seconds. Pour the matcha into a pre-warmed cup.
4. If you have a steam wand, steam your milk now. Pour warmed milk over the matcha, keeping the milk foam intact.
5. Add ice.

It's easy to see that Japanese tea lends itself to cold preparations. Each one of these recipes was designed to bring out the natural charm of the teas themselves without added herbs or flowers. But these recipes can also work as a jumping-off point for creating your own blends or "mocktails." When the quality of the tea is high and the recipe is prepared correctly, these cold teas can inspire all sorts of creativity. And how about adding some alcohol? Read on for a few ideas on how to use tea as a creative ingredient in a cocktail.

TEA AND ALCOHOL

Tea is a fascinating ingredient. And cocktails are made up of just that—fascinating ingredients. I first encountered tea and alcohol together in a drink—or perhaps infusion is the correct term—while visiting Shinya Sakurai at his eponymous tea atelier in Tokyo. I was struck by his understanding of the compelling characteristics of each of his teas. He could make a tea the star of a drink while using alcohol to complement, counterpoint, and ultimately enhance its best characteristics. It was the simplicity of his approach that struck me as well—with even just two compelling ingredients, he could achieve incredible harmony.

Tea is a remarkable companion to alcohol in that it can add both aromatics, through esters and oils, and depth, through catechins and amino acids. It can be floral, smoky, and oceanic. It can add rich savory umami, salinity, sweetness, or a sophisticated mouth-puckering astringency. Tea is astounding in its breadth and depth of exciting flavors and aromas. And Japanese tea specifically also offers something psychoactive: Theanine can beautifully counterbalance the giddy buzz of alcohol. With all of these incredible dimensions, I am always surprised that more people behind the bar are not celebrating this incredible plant by mixing it with alcohol.

The good news: There are plenty of talented people who have been inspired enough by tea to welcome it into their shakers and stirring glasses. Let's meet two of these specialists and see how tea has inspired them.

Interview

JIM MEEHAN

Jim Meehan's hospitality career spans twenty-five years. It began in Madison, Wisconsin, and took him to New York City and then Portland, Oregon, where he's working on his third book and opening a new restaurant with Submarine Hospitality called Takibi.

Zach Mangan: What surprises or inspiration has working with tea provided you?

Jim Meehan: Ever since I became acquainted with high-quality loose leaf teas at Gramercy Tavern in New York City back in 2005, I've been smitten with it. The variety of flavors, from peachy oolongs to grassy senchas to smoky lapsang souchongs, with seemingly everything in between, are a boon to bartenders.

Do you categorize tea more as an aromatic, textural, or flavor component when building a drink? Or all three?

All three. So much taste is aroma, and tea has so much character, which becomes airborne—through volatility—when it's served hot. Tea's tannins can provide textural grip on your palate and dry out sweeter ingredients in mixed drinks. Many teas have an oily, rich liquor that reminds me of white Burgundy.

Has anything from Japanese tea culture influenced how you make drinks in general?

Most Japanese bartenders will tell you that the style and grace that have become synonymous with their bars and bartending is inspired by the Japanese tea ceremony. I'm no expert in it, but from what I understand, the reverence for natural, elemental vessels and service ware spruced up with little more than flowers, in a quiet space with limited decorations to not distract from the tea makers' craft and facilitate appreciation of the tea, is wondrous. Bars are loud, boisterous, busy places and I'm always trying to find a calm, quiet space: even if it's in my head. I'm about as elegant as an aardvark, but I appreciate friends and colleagues who can pull this off behind the bar, and I do my best to bring the way of Japanese tea into my life where I can.

Recipe

JIM MEEHAN'S
EXCHANGE STUDENT

This combination of Japanese and American ingredients celebrates the respectful interplay and eternal learning between each country's makers and mixers in a classic toddy with a garnish that crowns the rim of the glass like the Hinomaru cresting the horizon.

INGREDIENTS
120 mL (4 fl. oz.) yanagi houjicha (freshly brewed)
22 mL (.75 fl. oz.) Hoshiko Original Ume Liqueur
15 mL (.5 fl. oz.) St. George California Shochu
15 mL (.5 fl. oz.) St. George Baller Single Malt Whisky
½ tsp. Okinawan Kokuto brown sugar

DIRECTIONS
1. Build in a pre-warmed toddy glass then stir until the sugar dissolves.
2. Garnish with half a blood-orange wheel.

Interview

SHINYA
SAKURAI

Originally a mixologist, Shinya Sakurai has been at the forefront of the contemporary Japanese tea movement since 2014. After honing his skills and aesthetics managing Tokyo's Higashiya Ginza and Yakumo Saryo, Sakurai-san went on to open his namesake tea atelier, designed by the genius architect Shinichiro Ogata. Tea, he discovered, was a template to express what he loved most: a connection to the fleeting feeling of the four seasons and a way to connect directly with his customers. And this is why we became quick friends—our mutual feeling of admiration for and freedom of expression with tea.

Zach Mangan: Can you tell me how you got your start?

Shinya Sakurai: I started with cocktails. I started as a bartender and did that for two years, and I got my previous job at Simplicity, a company that runs a Japanese confectionery shop called Higashiya. At first, fifteen years ago, I didn't know anything about tea, and I was mainly making cocktails as a bartender. And at that time we had the confectionery shop on the first floor and the cafe space on the second floor in the house-style building, and the cafe was functioning as a bar at night. There, you could enjoy whiskey and wine while having sweets, beans, daifuku, or yōkan. Of course, we made cocktails as well. And I started to learn about tea there. So I didn't start learning about tea voluntarily.

But you became more interested in tea as time went on?

Yes. While working with tea and cocktails I became more aware of the Japanese concept of shiki, admiring Japan's four seasons. Shiki is at the heart of Japanese cuisine as well. And I applied that to our menu. I was doing that while making tea and cocktails. Around that time I started to think that I must properly promote tea. Higashiya was opened in 2004, but not many people spent money on Japanese tea at that time. But after ten years, people had more of a desire to explore Japanese tea.

Unfortunately there was still no real place where you could drink and study Japanese tea at that time. So that made me have the desire to open my shop.

And once you opened you decided to implement your cocktail experience as well?

That's right. I came up with the idea that it might be fun to make the tea an alcoholic drink. I make things up like that. Then, various things get mixed up and something new including the new tastes will come out through tea.

Do you find tea and cocktails inform each other?

Well, tea and cocktails are similar for me. I'm talking about the movements and gestures. And both have recipes. The only difference is that this is an alcoholic beverage and we mix it with carbonated water, but the other is mixed with hot water. As many mixologists use the best fruits of the season for cocktails, I am making tea with the best ingredients of the season as well as the best tea of the season.

What is your desert-island tea?

Well, I would bring sencha, but among sencha, I would bring the one grown from the seedling (zairai).

Recipe

SHINYA SAKURAI'S SENCHA GIN

This infusion is a deep and refined expression of sencha. It can be enjoyed ice-cold in a thin-walled glass or can serve as a base for your own cocktail creation.

DIRECTIONS

1. Combine 20 g deep-steamed sencha, preferably Saemidori (we recommend our Chiran Sencha or Asa No Yume Tamaryokucha) with 750 mL (25 fl. oz.) gin. Steep for twenty-four hours in the refrigerator then strain well.
2. Add 10 g light-steamed sencha (we like our Uji No Sato) to the gin and allow to steep refrigerated for 48 hours. Strain the leaves well.
3. Serve chilled or over one large ice cube.
4. Store remainder in the refrigerator.

CHAPTER ELEVEN

Tea and Food

At this point, the comparisons of tea to wine may be getting redundant. But when talking about pairing tea and food—as hard as one tries, there's just no escaping it. The fact is, tea is not only an incredible beverage for drinking alongside food—it also acts as a remarkable ingredient. When used, it can add new dimensions to both savory and sweet dishes. In the chapter ahead, I discuss the intersection of tea and food with food professionals and lay out a few pairings and recipes that highlight the incredible potential for tea in a new and exciting context.

Tea in Japan has always been served in the company of food. The long-form tea ceremony is accompanied by a kaiseki meal. A steaming cup of konacha, a form of powdered green tea, is often served alongside the most pristine nigiri sushi. Matcha soft serve is available at every rest stop from Hokkaido to Kagoshima. In a sense, the taste of tea developed alongside food and the inspiration has always gone both ways. Early tea cafes called kissaten were drinking establishments that served tea, food, and alcohol to weary travelers in old Japan. The simple dishes were always served with hot tea and hot sake and the flavors had to be congruent. No garlic. No cheese. But miso, dashi, and soy sauce fit perfectly with the roasted aroma of houjicha and the mild umami of bancha. And kaiseki, Japan's most delicate and sophisticated seasonal cooking style, developed to support the chanoyu tea ceremony. Kaiseki's seasonality, its manner of service, and its ceramics all grew out of the culture of tea.

In a discussion of tea as an ingredient, there is probably no better example than the tea-flavored sweets that are synonymous with Japan. When I asked a kiosk clerk at Narita International Airport what their top-selling candy was for foreigners returning home, the answer was the matcha Kit Kat. And if you browse the high-end patisseries of Ginza, Aoyama, or the backstreets of Kyoto, you'll find houjicha and matcha in some of the best bakers' most refined creations. The fragrance, flavor, and color of tea is just so well suited for sweets.

But tea also makes an excellent ingredient in savory dishes. And perhaps no dish defines the marriage of tea and cuisine as much as ochazuke, or tea poured over rice. According to Gurunavi, Japan's leading restaurant guide, "Ochazuke has a long history, and has been enjoyed in Japan for over a thousand years. As far back as the Heian period (794–1185), people began pouring hot water and tea over cooked rice. During the Edo period (1603–1867), drinking green tea became more widespread and many began to prepare ochazuke with tea in place of water." Today ochazuke can be prepared in adventurous and delicious ways incorporating sashimi, pickles, seaweed, and vegetables, making for a simple, hearty, and delicious meal.

Let's take a look at a few winning combinations of tea and food you can try at home.

TEA PAIRINGS

While tea makes a great ingredient, it can also be fun and rewarding to pair teas with food. I have had so much fun working with chefs to come up with exciting tea pairings to accentuate the nuances of their dishes. I think of tea as having the ability to do three things in a pairing: The first is completing a dish. A tea completes a dish when its flavors harmonize with the food. The second is creating contrast. Tea can offer both flavor and temperature contrasts, which can lead to a unique dining experience. The last is augmenting a meal. A tea *(continued on p. 187)*

Recipe

HAYASHI HIROHISA'S OCHAZUKE

With family roots in the restaurant industry going back more than one hundred years, beginning with his great, great grandfather in Echizen, chef Hayashi Hirohisa was born into a culinary world. Now considered a master of the kappo style, Hirohisa-san received a Michelin star in 2014. The list of ingredients he is known for reads like a complete menu of Japan: fish, fowl, game, and vegetables; steamed, fried, grilled, and raw. Hirohisa-san is also a passionate lover of sake—he is a certified sake sommelier—and tea. He was kind enough to share his recipe for traditional ochazuke.

INGREDIENTS

60 g (½ cup) steamed rice

Prepared fish or pickled plum (see below for preparation)

150 mL (5 fl. oz.) houjicha or sobacha tea

1 shiso leaf (cut or torn off)

½ square of nori (seaweed), shredded

1 Japanese rice cracker

Sesame seeds

Wasabi (to taste)

DIRECTIONS

1. Place steamed rice in a small bowl.
2. Place prepared fish or pickled plum over the rice.
3. Place shiso, nori, sesame seeds, and
    rice cracker on top.

Option One

GRILLED SALMON

Season a small piece (30 g / 1 oz.) of salmon with salt and broil or bake at 400–415°F for four to five minutes.

Option Two

GRIMADAI

Use raw madai (sea bream) or another white fish such as fluke or sea bass.

   Combine 100 mL (3.5 fl. oz.) each of sake, mirin, and soy sauce. Cook over low heat until alcohol begins to evaporate, roughly two minutes. Allow the mixture to cool, then mix with 1 teaspoon of sesame seeds to form a coarse paste. Add the cut fish (40 g / 1.5 oz., or 4 very small pieces) to the mixture and marinate for ten minutes.

Option Three

PICKLED PLUM

Pit 1 plum and slice finely with a knife.

Recipe

YOSHIE SHIRAKAWA'S MATCHA & HOUJICHA COOKIES

Yoshie Shirakawa is an award-winning pastry chef from Japan. Shirakawa-san was a culinary school instructor in Tokyo in the early stages of her career. As her experience grew, she set her sights on New York City, where she eventually became the executive pastry chef of several restaurants and bakeries. In 2018, Shirakawa-san achieved her dream of opening her own bakery, Pâtisserie Fouet, a patisserie by day and dessert bar by night. At Fouet, which means "whisk," Shirakawa-san showcases her unique spin on conventional cuisine, introducing innovative French desserts and pastries with Japanese ingredients and flair.

Recipe

MATCHA COOKIES

INGREDIENTS

210 g all-purpose flour

20 g Kettl Hukuju Matcha

2 g sea salt

165 g unsalted butter (room temperature)

115 g powdered sugar

50 g granulated sugar

DIRECTIONS

1. Whisk together all-purpose flour, Hukuju Matcha, and sea salt. Mix in a large bowl and sift.
2. In a separate bowl, beat unsalted butter until creamy. Add powdered sugar and beat until just combined.
3. Add dry ingredients to the bowl and mix until incorporated.
4. Divide and shape dough into two 11.5″ x 1″ (30 cm x 2.5 cm) rolls. Tightly wrap each roll in parchment paper and refrigerate for a minimum of two hours.*
5. Unwrap dough from parchment paper and roll in granulated sugar.
6. Cut rolls into 0.5″ (1.25 cm) slices and place onto a parchment lined sheet pan.
7. Bake at 350°F for eleven minutes or until edges brown.

*Dough can be stored in the freezer and defrosted and sliced thirty minutes prior to baking.

Recipe

HOUJICHA COOKIES

INGREDIENTS

130 g all-purpose flour

65 g almond flour

8 g Kettl houjicha powder

1 g sea salt

20 g egg yolk

2 g vanilla paste

20 g granulated sugar

115 g unsalted butter (room temperature)

45 g additional granulated sugar

50 g powdered sugar

DIRECTIONS

1. Whisk together all-purpose flour, almond flour, houjicha powder, and sea salt. Mix in a large bowl and sift.
2. In a separate bowl, mix together egg yolk, granulated sugar (20 g), and vanilla paste.
3. Beat unsalted butter until creamy and add remaining granulated sugar (45 g). Once combined, add egg yolk, granulated sugar (20 g), and vanilla paste mixture and beat well.
4. Add dry ingredients to bowl and mix until incorporated.
5. Divide and shape the dough into two 11.5" x 1" (30 cm x 2.5 cm) oval rolls. Tightly wrap each roll in parchment paper and refrigerate for a minimum of two hours.
6. Unwrap dough from parchment paper.
7. Cut rolls into 0.5" (1.25 cm) slices and place onto parchment lined sheet pan.
8. Bake at 350°F for thirteen minutes or until edges turn brown.
9. Remove from oven and dust with powdered sugar to finish.

Recipe

MATCHA ICE CREAM

It is perhaps the most iconic of all Japanese tea sweets: matcha ice cream. In our shops we serve a wonderful version crafted by the folks at Il Laborotorio Del Gelato, a gelateria based here in New York City. The recipe below served as both the inspiration and template for the product we sell. The secret: lots of matcha. You will notice this has a deep, rich color and heady fragrance.

INGREDIENTS

3 egg yolks
16 g matcha powder, sifted
150 mL (5.25 fl. oz.) heavy cream
100 mL (3.5 fl. oz.) whole milk
75 g sugar

DIRECTIONS

1. Combine the egg yolks and sugar in a bowl and mix well for
    a few minutes. You want the yolks and sugar to fall in "ribbons"
    from the whisk—this is a sign the texture is where it needs
    to be.

2. In a separate bowl, combine the heavy cream, whole milk,
    and sifted matcha and gently stir until they are fully integrated,
    making sure any clumps of matcha have been worked out.

3. Combine all ingredients from both bowls, mix well, and pour
    into either an ice cream maker or a cold metal bowl. If you
    do not have an ice cream maker, put the metal bowl with ice
    cream into the freezer and allow to sit for several hours. If
    you do have an ice cream maker, allow it to mix for about
    twenty to twenty-five minutes, or until mixture has solidified.
    Once the texture is correct, transfer the matcha ice cream
    to the freezer for several hours.

augments a meal when its flavors combine with the flavors of the dish and both seem to change. Augmenting a dish with tea can be tricky, but when done successfully the results are remarkable.

There are no hard or fast rules with pairing. The key is to experiment and see what works—and of course, what doesn't. Below are a few ideas to get you started.

SIMPLE PAIRINGS

- Pair hot iribancha with bagels, smoked salmon, cream cheese, capers, and onion.
- Pair sparkling oolong "champagne" with fried chicken.
- Pair mizudashi sencha with fresh mango.
- Pair hot houjicha with kettle corn.
- Pair gyokuro with fresh sea urchin or oysters.

Creativity and exploration are key to coming up with remarkable dishes and winning pairings. My hope is that this chapter will lead you to develop your own creations.

CHAPTER TWELVE

Tea and Health

IF YOU TYPE THE WORDS *GREEN* AND *TEA* INTO GOOGLE, THE predictive text that appears after is "health benefits." I'd wager most people have heard that green tea is good for you. Beyond that, things get vague. You might have wondered: Exactly how does tea support health? Are all green teas healthy? How much green tea should I consume for better health? Is my tea provider over-promising on the benefits of the tea they sold me? These are all things I've wanted answers to myself. Here, I share the information I've learned about the power of the tea and its effects on our health.

The topic of tea's health benefits is fraught with mistruths, misleading statements, and frustrating generalizations. So I turned to health-and-wellness expert Dr. Andrew Weil for answers to some of my questions. I could think of few better individuals to help untangle fact and fiction.

Interview

DR. ANDREW WEIL

Dr. Andrew Weil is a world-renowned leader and pioneer in the field of integrative medicine, a healing-oriented approach to health care, which encompasses body, mind, and spirit.

Combining a Harvard education and a lifetime of practicing natural and preventive medicine, Dr. Weil is the founder and director of the Andrew Weil Center for Integrative Medicine at the University of Arizona, where he also holds the Lovell-Jones Endowed Chair in Integrative Rheumatology and is clinical professor of medicine and professor of public health.

Dr. Weil is internationally recognized as an expert on healthy lifestyles, known for his philosophy of healthy aging and his critique of the future of medicine and health care.

Just as Dr. Weil suggests, green tea is not a wonder drink that will solve all of your health problems or detox your system. While green tea is now sold in ready-to-drink bottles and pill and powder form, it is generally overhyped as a cure-all. And most of the time, the quality of the tea or tea supplement you are being sold is bottom of *(continued on p. 193)*

Zach Mangan: Let's jump right in with the question I am asked daily: "What are the health benefits of green tea?"

Dr. Andrew Weil: I think tea in general is a healthful beverage and I am tempted to say the healthiest form of caffeine you can ingest. While I believe all teas are healthy, green tea probably has more benefits than other types.

Do we have strong scientific evidence to prove the beneficial impact that green tea has on our health?

Most of the information we have comes from epidemiological studies. A very large study conducted in Japan several years ago showed that the mortality rate was lower in those who drank five or six cups of tea a day. This doesn't prove a cause-and-effect relationship, just suggests an association. The only way to prove a direct connection between green tea and health would be through prospective studies where you put people on green tea and watch what happens over time. Unfortunately, such studies haven't been conducted. We do know the effects of some of the constituents of green tea in the body, particularly epigallocatechin gallate (EGCG).

So, it would be interesting to see longer-term studies where people are looked at while drinking tea in order to understand the real impact.

Exactly, but that probably isn't going to happen because those are costly and difficult to organize. Based on what we know, we can say that drinking green tea regularly probably supports cardiovascular health, boosts defenses against cancer, and fortifies the body's antioxidant defenses. So, while we cannot make specific statements such as "green tea prevents heart disease" or "green tea prevents a specific form of cancer," we can infer some sort of health benefit from the many epidemiological studies and chemical analyses that have been conducted to date.

But you often see these highly targeted and specific claims of green tea being specifically good for weight loss or specifically good for a certain type of ailment or illness. Do you agree with the specificity that many green tea companies claim to sell their products?

Most of that is nonsense. Let's take matcha as an example. Matcha is the only form of tea where the whole leaf is consumed. And we know that the shading process of growing matcha increases the content of chlorophyll and flavor compounds—including flavonoids—which we know are beneficial for our health. Matcha probably has a higher content of those beneficial compounds than other forms of green tea.

There is a lot of predatory marketing around green tea. How can the consumer navigate that and weed out fact from fiction? Should buzzwords like "detox" or "superfood" be red flags?

Yes, I would see them as warning signs. Some people, like you, Zach, have done a great job of educating people. And my website, Matcha Kari, is trying to do the same.[1] But we still have a long way to go. A few years ago, if I ordered green tea in a high-end hotel, I was likely to get jasmine-flavored green tea; it was impossible to get really good sencha or gyokuro. I remember organizing a fundraising luncheon some time ago. I had planned the menu very carefully and I had bags of very good-quality sencha on the table. I suggested to a woman I was sitting with, "You should try this," and she replied, "We are big lovers of green tea, we've been into green tea for years." When she dipped the bag into the hot water in her cup she exclaimed, "Wow, this is green!" So it really is that level of not knowing. We still have a lot of work to do.

It is so true. So many people just haven't been introduced to good-quality great tea. And I hear it again and again: "Oh my God, I didn't know tea could taste like that."

In medical practice over the years I've seen so many people who are physically addicted to coffee and have physical problems related to their coffee intake; often, they don't make the connection. I am talking physical problems like irregular heartbeats, indigestion, urinary problems, anxiety, and insomnia. I rarely see tea do that or cause the kind of physical addiction so common with coffee. I believe the quality of caffeine stimulation from green tea is different from that of coffee and probably better for you.

Absolutely. I find the caffeine from coffee to affect me much differently—an absolutely racing feeling.

Exactly, and there are also very different cultural meanings around the two. Coffee has a long history of association with political radicalism and argumentativeness while tea is associated with meditation and contemplation. That also is a point for tea in my mind.

Are there any conditions or diseases that would benefit most specifically from drinking green tea?

Green tea has a modest effect in lowering cholesterol as long as you combine it with a healthy diet. It also has anti-inflammatory effects, and I always recommend it as part of an anti-inflammatory diet. So, while I would be reluctant to recommend green tea for specific conditions or diseases, it is fair to say that green tea is supportive of health. Its content of flavonoids and antioxidants helps support immune and cardiovascular function and strengthens the body's defenses.

Some people are highlighting the benefits that some components in green tea, mainly catechin, could have in fighting COVID-19. Is there any scientific evidence?
Two recent papers reported that EGCG, one of the main components in green tea, may actually inhibit the entry of the virus into cells. While that is an interesting finding, you cannot conclude that drinking green tea is going to protect you from getting the disease. It may make you more resistant to COVID-19 infection.

Aside from the nutritional components of tea, do you think the ritual or communal aspect of drinking tea has also a positive psychological impact?
I do. I think sharing the preparation and consumption of tea can be a very good social ritual, especially in these times.

the barrel. And the companies that promote their tea this way are doing it for one reason: to sell it to you. But even in spite of all the noise and false marketing, high-quality green tea is a powerful anti-inflammatory that is capable of supporting better health. And while I can tell you from experience that tea can enhance your health, I feel more comfortable sharing the latest clinical data. Read on to learn more.

CATECHINS

Green tea is a natural, healthy beverage that has been shown again and again in peer-reviewed research to have positive effects on the body and mind. The tea plant contains a full spectrum of health-supporting chemicals that likely work synergistically, but the most well understood are polyphenols, especially the polyphenols known as flavonoids. Among flavonoids, the subgroup called catechins, a family of powerful antioxidants, is by far the most well researched. The four main catechins that occur in green tea are (-)-epicatechin (EC), (-)-epicatechin-3-gallate (ECG), (-)-epigallocatechin (EGC), and (-)-epigallocatechin-3-gallate (EGCG).[2] Of these catechins, EGCG and EGC are found in the highest amounts in green tea and have been the subject of the most studies. These catechins have been shown to demonstrate a variety of antimicrobial properties. Consumption of green tea has been shown to distribute these compounds and/or their metabolites throughout the body, which allows for not only the possibility of treatment of infections but also the prevention of infections.

Catechins are antimicrobial and have been shown to destroy many common bacteria and viruses in lab tests. So when they are consumed, it is possible that they can help to either destroy or dismantle common bacteria in the body, allowing its natural defenses to do the rest. The amount of catechin in your tea is directly related to the quality of the product. Teas made from first flush leaves that were processed and stored well have the highest levels of catechin. As we learned in the chapter on matcha, teas that are grown in full sunlight, such as sencha, convert more amino acids into catechin, making them great candidates if you are looking to increase your intake. Another tip: consuming green tea along with vitamin C has been shown to make the catechin more bioavailable in the body. In the winter I love satsuma mandarin oranges with a cup of sencha—a common breakfast in Shizuoka. Not only do they taste great together, but they work together in the body to promote health— certainly the intelligence of nature at work.

GREEN TEA: A NATURAL ANTI-INFLAMMATORY

In addition to acting as an antimicrobial agent, catechin in green tea also works as a powerful anti-inflammatory. Studies have shown promising results for green tea use in treating irritable bowel syndrome[3] and collagen-induced arthritis in mice,[4] and it is thought to be beneficial for patients with a variety of conditions such as cancer, obesity, diabetes, cardiovascular disease, and neurodegenerative diseases.[5]

And it seems that these benefits are most concentrated in green tea when compared to other styles of tea such as black tea or oolong. An in-vitro study published in the *Journal of Advanced Pharmaceutical Technology & Research* concluded that while both green and black teas have anti-inflammatory effects, green tea's effects are more substantial, in all likelihood due to its higher flavonoid contents.[6] While it can be hard to say matter-of-factly that green tea can target any specific disease, an article in *Arthritis Research & Therapy* found EGCG to have promising effects on those suffering from rheumatoid arthritis.[7]

Perhaps the most overlooked and understudied health effects of tea drinking are the restorative mental health benefits that can come with it. The health benefits derived from the culture and practice of drinking tea are plentiful but rarely if ever discussed in medical journals or research papers. Meditation, breath awareness, and contemplative practices have been shown time and time again to calm the mind, lower heart rate and blood pressure, and promote a positive outlook. Tea, by nature, requires an investment of time and attention, and can be a catalyst for contemplation. The process starts with putting on the water, opening the tea and scooping it into the pot, waiting for the water to boil, pouring the water over the leaves, and watching them unfurl as they brew. Then there's the first sip and the contemplation that follows. Perhaps one of tea's most positive impacts on human health is the ritual it imposes—calming the mind and creating space in a hectic schedule. Our time with tea, however short, promotes a sense of calm well-being that can have ripple effects not only on our state of mind but perhaps also on our physical selves.

Humans, being social animals, benefit from time spent with others. Whether it's served at a child's tea party or a traditional Japanese tea ceremony, tea has brought people together for centuries. This "leisure time" might be better for us than we know. Studies have shown that human interaction lowers stress, positively modulates our immune systems, has a positive effect on cortisol levels, and can even prolong life. Perhaps a cup of tea among friends is just what the doctor ordered.

1. www.matcha.com
2. Wanda C. Reygaert, "Green Tea Catechins: Their Use in Treating and Preventing Infectious Diseases," *BioMed Research International* (July 2018): https://doi.org/10.1155/2018/9105261.
3. Fei-Yan Fan et al., "Catechins and Their Therapeutic Benefits to Inflammatory Bowel Disease," *Molecules* 22, no. 3 (March 2019): 484, https://doi.org/10.3390/molecules22030484.
4. M. Trekli et al., "Anti-inflammatory actions of green tea catechins and ligands of peroxisome proliferator-activated receptors," *International Journal of Experimental Pathology* 85, no. 4 (August 2004): 75, https://doi.org/10.1111/j.0959-9673.2004.390ap.x.
5. Tomokazu Ohishi et al., "Anti-inflammatory Action of Green Tea," *Anti-Inflammatory & Anti-Allergy Agents in Medicinal Chemistry* 15, no. 2 (2106): 74–90, https://doi.org/10.2174/1871523015666160915154443.
6. Priyanka Chatterjee et al., "Evaluation of anti-inflammatory effects of green tea and black tea: A comparative in vitro study," *Journal of Advanced Pharmaceutical Technology & Research* 3, no. 2 (Spring 2012): 136–138, https://doi.org/10.4103/2231-4040.97298.
7. Salahuddin Ahmed, "Green tea polyphenol epigallocatechin 3-gallate in arthritis: progress and promise," *Arthritis Research & Therapy* 12, no. 2 (2010): 208, https://doi.org/10.1186/ar2982.org/10.4103/2231-4040.97298.

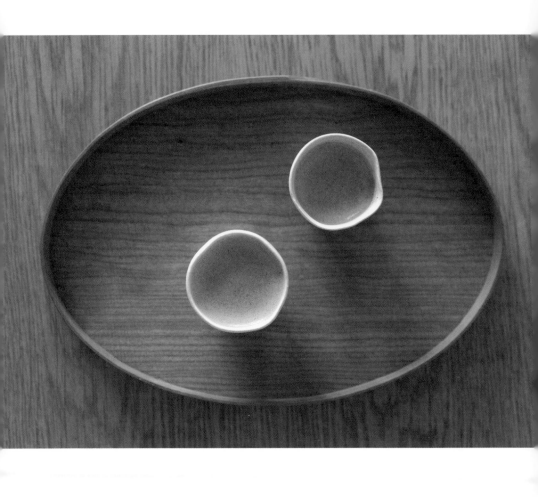

CHAPTER THIRTEEN

Tea and Caffeine

A QUESTION WE ARE OFTEN ASKED AT THE SHOP IS: DOES GREEN tea have caffeine? If so, how much? A simple question. Not such a simple answer. What makes this seemingly straightforward query a bit hard to answer is this: Asking how much caffeine is in green tea is like asking how much alcohol is in red wine. The answer can vary dramatically depending on the specific product in question. Note that the guidelines below are just that—guidelines—and will not be correct 100 percent of the time. We like to avoid speaking in certainties when it comes to something as complex as tea.

Does green tea have caffeine? Yes, but…All products made from *Camellia sinensis*, the plant responsible for tea, contain some caffeine. Sencha, for example, tends to contain 3 to 4 percent caffeine by dry weight. The *Camellia sinensis* plant produces a complex array of chemicals, caffeine among them. The presence of caffeine in the plant deters many of the insects that would snack on its leaves—essentially acting as a natural pesticide. The amount of caffeine that ends up in your cup depends on many factors, including the way your tea was grown, processed, and prepared.

The chemical composition of different teas can vary greatly depending on where and how they are grown. For example, teas that are grown without robust pesticides tend to produce more caffeine, since they need to fend for themselves against bugs. This is one of the reasons organic teas often have a more bitter profile (caffeine presents on the palate as bitter). Many higher-elevation senchas from Shizuoka (Honyama, Kawane, Shimizu) are grown in a hands-off manner and tend to have a brisk minerality and a soft astringency that is a result, in part, of elevated levels of caffeine.

How a tea is cultivated also impacts its caffeine content. For example, shaded teas like gyokuro, kabuse, and matcha are covered prior to harvesting. When a tea is covered, more of its naturally occurring theanine remains in the leaf. Theanine slows the absorption of caffeine into the bloodstream; so while shaded teas may not contain less caffeine, they can be less irritating to those with a caffeine sensitivity.

Interestingly, certain tea cultivars simply produce more caffeine than others naturally, in the same way that apples differ in color and flavor from one variety to the next.

TEA PROCESSING AND ITS IMPACT ON CAFFEINE

As we have learned, after tea leaves are picked they are quickly steamed to halt oxidation. Tea leaves can be steamed from ten seconds or so (asamushi) to forty-five seconds or more (fukamushi). The duration impacts the amount of caffeine that remains in the leaf. Caffeine is water soluble and can break down when exposed to steam. So it makes sense that when a tea is steamed for longer it can have slightly lower levels of caffeine. The same logic holds for teas that are roasted after processing, like houjicha. Houjicha goes through a secondary roasting process much like coffee—and the heat applied to the leaf causes some of the caffeine to leech out. So if you are looking for an option with less caffeine, houjicha is a great choice. You can lightly roast your tea leaves at home too—just heat a dry skillet and toast over medium heat for about one minute.

CAFFEINE LEVELS AND BREWING TEMPERATURE

While you can't control farming or processing techniques, you can control how you brew, which partly determines how much caffeine ends up in your cup. Caffeine, as previously mentioned, is water soluble, and is released more quickly in very hot water. If you are looking to limit caffeine, brew in water below 180°F (82°C). We can assume that roughly 5–6 grams of sencha brewed at 180°F (82°C) will release about 60–80 milligrams of caffeine.

The takeaway here is that all tea from the plant *Camellia sinensis* contains caffeine—even green tea. Generally, the higher quality and fresher your tea is, the more caffeine it will contain. If you are sensitive to caffeine, we recommend that you try any tea you are unfamiliar with earlier in the day, to see how it makes you feel.

ACKNOWLEDGMENTS

Thank you to my wife, Minami, my parents, Michalene and Tom, and my sisters, Sarah and Maggie, for your unwavering support. Thank you to Ethan Rafii, Derek Feldman, Miles Dugan, Stephanie Terasaki, and our entire Kettl NYC team. Thank you to Tokitsu-san, Kawaguchi-san, and Mouri-san of our Kettl Japan team.

Thank you to David Bouley, Andrew Weil, and Jim Meehan.

Thank you to my Yoshinoen Kurume family, and to all of our producers who supply us with the finest tea I have ever tasted. To all those in Japan who have taken the time to guide me through the tea fields and factories, answer my long-winded questions, and share the incredible world of tea with me. And all those who shared the wisdom that allowed this book to be written.

Especially Shinya Sakurai, Shinya Yamaguchi, Jiro Katahira, Hirokazu Sugiura, the Furukawa family, Kiyoharu Tsuji, Shinki Yamashita, Masahiro Kuma, Seiji Ito, and all those who work tirelessly to move Japanese tea forward: farmers, producers, chefs, artisans, artists, and designers.

Thank you to our restaurant partners all over the world and our Kettl customers who trust us with something so important: their morning cup of tea.

Thank you to my editor, Jennifer Thompson, acquisitions editor Parker Menzimer, and the whole team at Princeton Architectural Press for believing in this book and helping me see it through.

WHERE AND HOW TO SHOP
FOR TEA IN JAPAN

Our customers often ask us to recommend our favorite tea shops in Japan. Here, we share a few of our favorite spots for tea and ceramics. We encourage you to visit if you find yourself in Tokyo, Kyoto, or Fukuoka.

Tokyo 東京

SAKURAI TEA EXPERIENCE

ADDRESS: 107-0062 Tokyo, Minamiaoyama, 5 Chome-6-23
PHONE: +81 03-6451-1539
WEBSITE: www.spiral.co.jp/en/shoplist/sakuraitea

Sakurai Tea Experience is one of our absolute favorite spots. This refined tea salon is run by our friend Shinya Sakurai and was designed by the genius architect and designer Shinichiro Ogata. This refined experience celebrates the minimal charm of contemporary Japanese design and offers a variety of ways to enjoy Japanese tea: a single order of tea, a flight, tea cocktails, or (our recommendation) a set menu with a light dining experience.

HIGASHIYA GINZA

ADDRESS: 104-0061 Tokyo, Chuo City, Ginza, 1 Chome-7-7
PHONE: +81 03-3538 3230
WEBSITE: www.higashiya.com/en/

Higashiya is a contemporary Japanese wagashi shop. Wagashi are traditional Japanese confections. Owned and designed by a master of design, Shinichiro Ogata (he also designed Sakurai Tea Experience), the space itself is astonishingly beautiful and brings an immediate sense of calm. Relax and order a light meal or sweets with a selection from an impressive list of Japanese teas.

OMOTESANDO CHA CHA NO MA

ADDRESS: 150-0001 Tokyo, Shibuya City, Jingumae, 5 Chome–13–14
PHONE: +81 03-5468-8846

Located in Omotesando, this cafe, run by Japanese tea specialist Yoshi Watada, is a haven for single-cultivar sencha. Watada-san has a unique sensibility and carries a vast collection of hard-to-find cultivars. His shop doesn't have the most inspiring atmosphere of all the places on this list, but just close your eyes and enjoy the inspired tea.

TOKYO SARYO

ADDRESS: 154-0011 Tokyo, Setagaya City, Kamiuma, 51 Chome–34–15
PHONE: +81 03-6805-3071
WEBSITE: www.tokyosaryo.jp

This cafe was started as a project for the owner's design group and gained popularity quite quickly. An ode to simplicity, Tokyo Saryo offers a selection of single-cultivar senchas in a minimalist setting. We love it because you can choose two cultivars from different regions and enjoy them side by side, instantly illuminating the breadth and depth of sencha as a category.

Kyoto 京都

RYUOUEN CHAHO

ADDRESS: 604-0935 Kyoto, Nakagyo Ward, 690 Nijo Dori
PHONE: +81 075-231-3693

Tucked along a backstreet—just around the corner from the famous Kyoto tea shop Ippodo—Ryuouen's products are sourced from Uji and sold directly to discerning Kyotoites and tea-ceremony schools, primarily the Omotesenke school. While you can't sit and have tea, a welcome cup will be served to you—and if Sugiura-san is working and you mention Kettl, you just might get a second cup. Stock up while you're here.

NISHINOTOIN TEA SHOP & TEA HOUSE

ADDRESS: 604-8277 Kyoto, Nakagyo Ward, Nishinotoin-dori Oike-dori West

PHONE: +81 075-223-0909

WEBSITE: www.marukyu-koyamaen.co.jp/english/motoan.html

This shop is matcha producer Maryukyu Koyamaen's Kyoto outpost. Nishinotoin occupies a quaint space with a view of a small outer garden. Sit and have tea (we recommend the special gyokuro selection made solely for this location) and then grab a houjicha or matcha soft serve on your way out the door.

TSUJI RIHEI HONTEN

ADDRESS: 611-0021 Kyoto Prefecture, Uji City, 41 Uji Wakamori

PHONE: +81 774-29-9021

WEBSITE: www.tsujirihei.co.jp/en/information/

Many places in Uji, a city thirty minutes from Kyoto by train, cater to tourists and primarily peddle sweets. But Tsuji Rihei Honten, a bit off the main drag, focuses on high-grade Uji tea. You can order a variety of senchas, gyokuros, matchas, and even tenchas. And the shop does in fact have wonderful sweets. We recommend going solo and enjoying the view of the garden.

Fukuoka 福岡

YOROZU

ADDRESS: 810-0042 Fukuoka, Chuo Ward, Akasaka, 2 Chome–3–32

PHONE: +81 092-724-7880

WEBSITE: www.yorozu-tea.jp

Yorozu is a small salon dedicated to tea, a hidden gem in the backstreets of Fukuoka. Much of the tea on the menu is sourced from producers in Yame, a city in Fukuoka Prefecture. Tokubuchi-san, the owner, is deft at crafting cocktails using tea, and his service is impeccable—perhaps a bit more showy than that of some other mixologists in Japan. We recommend you go after dinner for tea and (a few) cocktails.

YAME TEA AND JAPANESE GARDEN

ADDRESS: 810-0051 Fukuoka, Chuo Ward, Ohorikoen, 1 Chome-1-9

PHONE: +81 092-401-0275

WEBSITE: www.fukuoka-now.com/en ohori-terrace-yame-tea-and-japanese-garden/

Situated in Ohori Park in central Fukuoka, Yame Tea and Japanese Garden is a wonderful place to visit in the warmer months. Make sure to get a seat outside overlooking the park's expansive pond and enjoy a variety of teas from Yame— both cold and hot. Try the Yame matcha soft serve. Just order two—you'll thank me later.

Kagoshima 鹿児島

SUSUMUYA CHATEN

ADDRESS: 890-0052 Kagoshima, Uenosonocho, 2 Chome-7-13

PHONE: +81 099-251-4141

WEBSITE: www.susumuya.com

Susumuya Chaten is owned by Kotaro Shinbara, who is from a family of tea wholesalers that has operated in Kagoshima for over one hundred years. This cafe connects the business directly with consumers and fans of tea. On offer is a wide selection of single-cultivar senchas direct from the family's private stock. Make sure to try the matcha shaved ice—it's divine, even in winter!

Aichi Prefecture – prefecture of Japan famous for producing tencha

aracha – unrefined tea leaves

ara kanso – step one in the tencha drying process

asamushi – *aka* asamushicha, light-steamed tea (teas steamed about 15–20 seconds)

Baisao – a Japanese monk and tea seller who lived from 1675–1763

bocha – tea made from tea stalks

Camellia sinensis – Latinate name for the plant that produces tea

chanoyu – Japanese tea ceremony

chasen – bamboo matcha whisk

chasen naoshi – stand for chasen

chashaku – bamboo scoop

chashi – tea master blender

chashitsu – traditional Japanese tearoom

chawan – matcha tea bowl

chazutsu – tea caddy

chuumushi (*see* futsumushi)

daifuku – type of wagashi

daimyo – Japanese feudal ruler

daizukasu – soy-based fertilizer

dentou hon gyokuro – traditionally made authentic gyokuro

fukamushi – *aka* fukamushicha, heavily steamed sencha (sencha steamed longer than 45 seconds)

Fukuoka – capital city of Japan's Fukuoka Prefecture

furui – matcha sifter

futsumushi – "regular" steamed sencha

gaiwan – lidded tea cup for brewing tea

genmai – brown rice

genmaicha – green tea blended with brown rice

genmaimatcha – genmaicha blended with matcha

goishicha – fermented bancha from Shikoku island

guricha – curled-leaf sencha, also called tamaryokucha

gyokuro – fine Japanese green tea, shaded during cultivation

hicha – a lesser tea from outside of Toganoo, as determined by a tōcha player

hiire – final firing in shiagecha process

hinnpyoukai – tea product to be shown competitively

hishaku – bamboo water ladle

hojiki – *aka* hoiro, ceramic tool for roasting tea

honcha – a "real" tea from Toganoo as determined by a tōcha player

Honyama – tea-producing region in Shizuoka Prefecture

honzu – shading tea by traditional methods using straw

Hoshinomura – tea-producing region in Fukuoka

houjicha – *aka* hōjicha, roasted tea

ichibancha – *aka* shincha, first harvest green tea

ikebana - the Japanese art of flower arranging

Iruma – tea-producing region in Saitama Prefecture

Ise cha – tea from the area of Ise in Mie Prefecture

Joyomachi – village in the city of Yame known for sencha and gyokuro production

jūdan – competitive title meaning "tenth degree," or top level

jukusei – aging or ripening, the final stage before milling tencha or the release of gyokuro

kabuse – shaded sencha green tea

kaiseki – traditional Japanese cuisine born from the tea ceremony

Kakegawa – tea-producing town in Shizuoka Prefecture

kakusan reikyaku – tencha cooling process

kama – cast-iron cauldron for boiling water

kamairicha – a traditional method of pan-firing tea

kanreisha – synthetic shade covering for tencha and gyokuro

karamono – Chinese ceramics popular during the Kamakura period in Japan

Kawane – famous tea-producing region in Shizuoka Prefecture

kintsugi – method of repairing ceramics using lacquer and gold

kissaten – tea and coffee cafe

konacha – strong powdered tea made of small fragments of sencha leaves

kukicha houjicha – tea made from roasted sencha stems

kyusu – Japanese teapot

lapsang souchong – smoked Chinese tea

matcha – milled green tea powder

mingei – Japanese folk craft movement of the 1920s

mizudashi – Japanese style of cold brewing

Murata Shukō – founder of Japanese tea ceremony also credited with inventing wabi sabi

Nagatani Soen – inventor of sencha production

neri kanso – final drying step in tencha processing

nibancha – second harvest green tea

nijiriguchi – half-size door to a tearoom

ocha – Japanese word for *tea*

ochazuke – tea poured over rice

Okinawan kokuto – Japanese brown sugar

ooika – fragrance associated with Uji gyokuro

Saichou – ancient Japanese monk, first to plant tea

sanbancha – *aka* bancha, third harvest green tea

sencha – steamed green tea

Sen no Rikyū – Japanese tea master

seppuku – ritual suicide

shiagecha – refined tea

shiboridashi – small, filterless teapot

shiki – Japanese concept of admiring the seasons

Shimizu – a town in Shizuoka Prefecture

shincha – *aka*, ichibancha, first harvest of tea (literally "new tea")

shinkansen – Japanese bullet train

shinme – fresh young tea leaves

shizenshitate – unpruned tea plants used for tencha or gyokuro production

shogun – historical Japanese military dictator

shoin-style – a particular style of tearoom

shokunin – master craftsperson

shudei – clay popular in Tokoname tea pots

sobacha – buckwheat tea

Soen Nagatani – creator of sencha

Tai-an – famous tearoom designed by Sen no Rikyū

Takeno Jōō – a master of the tea ceremony and a well-known merchant during the Sengoku period

tatami – traditional Japanese floor mat

tana – coverings used to shade tencha or gyokuro

tencha – produced to be ground into matcha

Tenryū – tea-producing region in Shizuoka Prefecture

tetsubin – cast-iron tea kettle

tezumi – the process of hand-harvesting tea

theanine – an amino acid found in green tea

tōcha – historical tea-tasting betting game

Tokoname – Japanese city known for kyusu artisanry

Uji – Japanese city in Kyoto Prefecture

umami – savory flavor

Umegashima – mountainous tea-producing region of Shizuoka Prefecture

Ureshino – tea-producing city in Saga Prefecture

usucha – thin matcha preparation

wabi-cha – "simple tea"

wabi sabi – a style celebrating the rustic, simple and quiet

wagashi – Japanese sweets

yōkan – type of red bean wagashi

yuzamashi – spouted tea-cooling vessel

zairai – heirloom sencha grown from seed

ZACH
MANGAN

In 2010, Zach Mangan took a monthlong solo trip to Japan and realized that the freshest and most delicious Japanese tea products were not exported. Driven by a simple desire to connect incredible Japanese teas with an international audience, Mangan spent two years developing relationships with several of Japan's most notable tea producers. Thus, his company, Kettl, was born.

Mangan is known throughout Japan as an authority on Japanese tea. He has consulted for the Shizuoka Tea Association and studied tea production extensively at origin with producers in both Fukuoka and Uji. Mangan was a finalist and the first non-Japanese person to take top honors in the Zenkoku Gyokuro No Umai Irikata Contest, a nationwide gyokuro brewing competition in Japan. Mangan has been a contributor to radio, books, and magazines and has developed the tea menus for chefs holding a combined thirty-nine Michelin stars.

Based in both Fukuoka and Brooklyn, Mangan continues to create connections between Japan's most distinguished tea producers and tea drinkers throughout the world.

Instagram: www.instagram.com/kettltea/
Twitter: www.twitter.com/kettltea
Facebook: www.facebook.com/kettltea/